Praise for *Path of*

"Because the Creator gave each c
ing life, sometimes the Creator gives u
peoples that we can all share. With
generous teachings in this book."

Vi Hilbert, taq W seblu, Upper Skagit Elder and author of the *Lushootseed Dictionary* and *Haboo: Native American Stories from Puget Sound*

"I've known Robin Tekwelus Youngblood for many years as a teacher and healer, artist and friend. I have a lot of respect for her and her work. I've seen her work touch many people over the years, lifting people out of darkness and despair. This book will bring light and happiness to many."

Johnny Moses, "Whis.stem.men.knee" (Walking Medicine Robe); Tulalip traditional healer, spiritual leader and storyteller

"Sandy and Robin have given to others a true teaching of divine order and timing with their gentle approach to learning communication with Great Spirit. This teaching guides us in understanding connection, healing and flow. It is a true honor to know Sandy. I have deep respect for the work presented in these teachings."

Rhonda Meals, HD, PhD, Cherokee/Chickasaw, author of *Dancing with the Raven*, Co-founder of Spirits on the Wind Center

"Robin is a special sister to me. She comes from our area (the Coast Salish people). I'm really happy to know that Robin is brave enough to bring out these teachings to anyone with an open mind and heart in this time of great earth change."

Beaver Chief, Lummi Nation, Northwest Coast
Red Cedar Circle, Seattle, Washington

PATH of the
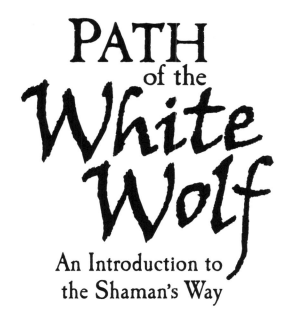

White Wolf

An Introduction to the Shaman's Way

Robin Tekwelus Youngblood

Sandy D'Entremont

PHOENIX PUBLICATIONS

ARDENVOIR, WA

PATH OF THE WHITE WOLF
An Introduction to the Shaman's Way

Published by
Phoenix Publications
P.O. Box 356
Ardenvoir, WA 98811

Art Direction and Interior Design by Robert Lanphear
Illustrations by Jason Oxrieder

Library of Congress Cataloging-in-Publication Data
Youngblood, Robin Tekwelus and D'Entremont, Sandy
Path of the white wolf: an introduction to the shaman's way/
Robin Tekwelus Youngblood and Sandy D'Entremont.
Library of Congress Control Number 2006934871
ISBN-10   0-9787954-0-7
ISBN-13   978-0-9787954-0-5
1. Native American 2. Spirituality 3. Shamanism
I. Title: Path of the White Wolf. II. Title
Second Printing

To the Healing of the Sacred
Hoop, and for All Our
Relations—Red, Yellow, Black,
and White. And to the spirits . . .
who are the real teachers.

Great Mystery,

We speak to you as your daughters, Robin and Sandy. We thank you for our lives and for this day. We thank you for the opportunity to do this work and to share these teachings in the world. Thank you for the beautiful abundance of our Mother Earth, she who holds us always. And thank you for the boundless inspiration of Father Sky and those who watch us always. Thank you for our teachers, those who have touched our lives in both body and spirit from all Earth's families, those who live on in our hearts and whose messages we are honored to carry forward with prayers for the seventh generation. And thank you for our students, who teach us more than they could possibly imagine. Thank you for our ancestors, who have given away so that we can be here in this time and place on the Wheel of Life. Thank you for our families, our partners, our children and grandchildren, those of blood and those of spirit, who bring incredible love and joy into our lives, and who also catch us when we falter, inspire us when we are disillusioned, encourage us when we are tired, and love us anyway. And finally, Great Mystery, from the bottom of our hearts, we thank you for allowing us to share this earthwalk together, as sisters of the wind, sisters of the heart, and for bringing us together to dance in partnership on this Red Road. We do this work for All Our Relations.

Aho Mitakuye Oyasin!

Contents

You have noticed that everything an Indian
does is in a circle, and that is because
the Power of the World always works in
circles, and everything tries to be round
. . . The sky is round, and I have heard
that the earth is round like a ball, and so
are all the stars. The wind, in its greatest
power, whirls. Birds make their nests in
circles, for theirs is the same religion as
ours . . . Even the seasons form a great
circle in their changing, and always come
back again to where they were. The life
of a man is a circle from childhood to
childhood, and so it is in everything where
power moves.

Black Elk (1863-1950): Oglala Sioux holy man

Finding the Path Home

nd so you find yourself stepping onto the Path of the White Wolf to depart on a life-changing journey. Where you go on this journey will be as diverse and powerful and beautiful as the Great Mystery itself. We will not try to predict what you will discover or the new understandings you will gain. Instead, we invite you to place your foot on a path many others have taken, a path of personal exploration and transformation. This path will manifest in ways that are uniquely yours, fashioned and shaped by your own perspectives and challenges, led and protected by your personal spirit guides and totems.

Everyone knows each journey begins with a single step. We begin this journey with the story of a traveler who, like many others, finds himself lost in his own homeland. He meets a White Wolf, which, as you will see, turns out to be the first of many.

Our grandfathers tell of a time hundreds of years ago—or perhaps just yesterday—when there lived a few two-leggeds who understood the languages of All Our Relations. From those times, comes a story of a man named Hears Much, who lived much like any other man—except that he was extraordinarily gifted with the art of language and understanding.

Hears Much was a hunter who lived in a village with his people. His Medicine was the ability to listen deeply to all Earth's children. When Blue Jay spoke to Deer to announce where Cougar took his morning walk, Hears Much spread a word of warning throughout the village. And when Mouse spoke to Trout about her busy quest to save seeds for winter, Hears Much reminded his people to store food. Hears Much not only understood the animals but also learned the language of wind and cloud, so that he knew when storm or sun approached. He stilled his mind to hear the words of the Stone People to find the valley where arrowhead flint lay. He listened to the song of the waters to know when drought might visit the land.

Although Hears Much loved his people, he preferred the company of wild things and spent much time away, his long stride taking him across mountain and valley. But always he returned home.

One day in his travels Hears Much became lost—which was very strange because he was an exceptional tracker. Trotting alone across a small river valley, he came upon a White Wolf sitting by the path. White Wolf spoke to the man and said, "How would you like to smoke the sacred Pipe with me?"

Hears Much thanked White Wolf and said, "Of course. I am honored that you would ask me to join you!"

The two sat together in the grass of a nearby meadow and smoked the sacred Pipe. When they finished, White Wolf said to him, "Because you have smoked my Pipe, you are my friend and my brother. My family will not harm you. I will take you to meet my people. They will be glad to know that you have smoked my Pipe and will speak to you."

Hears Much accompanied White Wolf across the valley and up the ridge. After awhile they met many Wolves. The Chief, a large White Wolf named Red Paws, called the other Wolves into Council. "Let us sit and hear what our brothers have to say," he said.

White Wolf stood and addressed the Council. He said, "This man is my brother. He smoked my Pipe and has agreed to visit and learn from us. Let us teach him our traditions."

The Wolf Council rolled in the dust and shook themselves, howling and growling. They showed their teeth and blinked their yellow eyes. Hears Much was fearful for a moment, but his White Wolf friend stayed close by his side.

Red Paws snapped his jaws at the Council, making his decision. "And so we shall," he agreed.

The Wolves guided Hears Much through the forest and down by the river, showing him tribes of Medicine Plants. Red Paws said, "We show you this root, and if any two-legged is bitten by a snake, give him this medicine. He will get well and drift not into the spirit world. The other Medicine Plants are useful for many two-legged pains and sicknesses." The Wolf Council gathered around Hears Much and explained the use of all the Medicine Plants—each member freely sharing his wisdom.

Next a Gray Wolf with blue eyes stood up and rolled on the ground. As he shook the dust from his fur, the other Wolves grew silent, showing great respect for this elderly brother. He handed Hears Much a deer-hoof rattle, explaining, "When a member of your two-legged family is sick, slipping into sleep too often, shake these Spirit-callers and the sick one will be returned to you and made well." The Wolf Council yipped with agreement, rolling on the ground to scratch their backs.

Suddenly a Wolf black as a shadow approached Hears Much. "Wolf Brother," said Black Wolf, handing Hears Much a piece of bone etched with a Wolf skull. "Hold this bone to your forehead if an enemy attempts to harm you. The power of night lives in the bone and will hide you so that you can overcome any ill intent your enemies throw at you." The Wolf Council howled in harmony, pointing their noses to the rising moon.

When the Wolf singers were silent, Hears Much spoke. He held his hand to his heart, showing his deep respect and appreciation for all the Council had shared. "I thank you, Wolf brothers. You are my teachers. I am glad I followed the White Wolf to your Council Lodge. Your words and wisdom fill my heart, and with your permission I will bring these teachings home to my people. But alas, I do not know the way back." The Wolf Council growled with understanding, closing their eyes to sleep.

The next day White Wolf guided Hears Much back to his homeland. Stopping just out of sight of the main village path, White Wolf said, "Take this bird-bone whistle. When you get close to your village, blow it. The Wolf Council will hear it and know you have been reunited with your people." Hears Much did as he was told, blowing the whistle as he entered the village. In the distance he heard the Wolf Council howling their acknowledgment and friendship.

Hears Much rested in his home, enjoying the sounds and smells of his village and the laughter of his two-legged friends. He did not know how to tell his family that he had become lost—of all things!—and met a White Wolf. But after several days he heard of a child who was ill, so he went to her. With the new healing powers he learned from the Wolf Council, he was able to cure the girl, bringing her back to her family and into harmony. And so began the journey of the first healer, a servant of the people, a seeker and a listener, a traveler finding the path home.*

*Common to the oral tradition in many cultures, the same stories are often found in geographically disparate parts of the continent. Although the language and words may be different, and details change naturally with time and repetition, the bones of the story—the medicine of the message—remains. In our memory, we've heard this story in varying formats many times, often credited to the Pawnee nation. We retell it here with appreciation for the storytellers who give us, among other things, the gift of remembering. These days we are most fortunate to have at our fingertips a handy convenience wisely named the World Wide Web, where you can find another version of this story entitled "The First Healer," recounted by Neshoba.

Returning to the Earth Mother

In today's world, many of us feel fractured spiritually and, perhaps, physically and mentally as well, due to the imbalances imposed by modern life. We yearn for connection and purpose, and try in frustration to find heart and meaning in work, relationships, and spirituality.

The Path of the White Wolf introduces you to the spiral road to wholeness and knowledge, a journey that reconnects you to your innate spirituality and to our loving Earth Mother. As you walk this road, you discover your heart's desire and your reason for incarnating into physical form. You find your connection to All Your Relations—animal, plant, and mineral—and recognize the next steps to take in your evolution as a spiritual being. The Spiral Path offers deep transformation via the blended use of contemporary and traditional indigenous practices. It reveals the interconnected, interdependent nature of all Earth's children, and dismantles the illusion of separation. Walking this path restores the harmonic balance common to the lifeways of our tribal ancestors.

The journey you are about to take is grounded in reverence for your connection to the Earth Mother. Accompanied by your teacher, White Wolf, you will explore a series of circular teachings, as each one builds upon another. Wolf shows you that within the wilderness of your soul, you are a divine spark from the Source, capable of much—perhaps more than you realize. As you *re-member* yourself to be a servant of Creation and reassemble the pieces of your life that have meaning and purpose, you will develop healing lifeways to replace patterns that do not support you. You will find a more empowered way of being. The Spiral Path we explore will help you transform habits that block your growth, habits such as negative thoughts, unsupported personal beliefs, unresolved emotional attachments, unhealthy or dysfunctional behavior patterns, and psychic wounds.

Under White Wolf's guidance, you will build a foundation that integrates timeless philosophical concepts as well as past, present, and future experiences. This integration helps you make sense of your spiritual evolutionary processes and allows you to recognize and understand the lessons that spirit gives you.

Wolf Medicine is that of the teacher, the pathfinder, the mentor. Wolves epitomize our innate wild spirit, tempered by a deep sense of family. Wolves are infinitely individualistic, yet loyal to the death. Their senses of hearing and smell are exquisitely keen. They cannot be fooled: they always sense truth. Wolves are intelligent and avoid trouble whenever possible. They are nocturnal—the classic image of the lone wolf standing atop a moonlit ridge links the wolf timelessly to the moon's psychic energies, to secret knowledge and wisdom.

For thousands of years White Wolf has guided people of wisdom. Okanagon chiefs who inhabited the central Columbia Plateau of British Columbia and Central Washington claimed him as totem; the Cherokee nation of the Eastern United States considered White Wolf to be their teacher and guide.

Those who follow White Wolf are leaders who understand responsibility and wield authority wisely. They are not afraid of commitment to a cause or of taking action to manifest their vision and deepest heart's desire. White Wolf's path is for those who understand that their life work is more than a day-to-day exercise in survival. It is for those who see the need to heal the Sacred Hoop (the energy that encompasses all beings and the Earth) and want to walk in balance with All Our Relations: two-legged, four-legged, winged ones, swimming ones, creepy-crawlers, standing people, stone people, the elementals, star beings, and our own Earth Mother.

The Spiral Path of the White Wolf connects you with a powerful medicine teacher who encourages you to be fully yourself and at the same time to fully connect with community. As Wolf guides you on the Spiral Path, all manner of things come to your attention in a new way.

Traveling The
Seven Sacred Directions

Each of the sacred directions—East, South, West, North, Above, Below, and Center—holds teachings that speak to us on a four-dimensional level: spiritual, physical, emotional, and mental. We must engage with all these levels to move and build from lesson to lesson, to learn and to change. Fully absorbed, we begin to recall the ways of our ancestors for whom peaceful, abundant coexistence was not only possible but necessary and, also, normal.

Path of the White Wolf

We dedicate one chapter to each of the Seven Directions. Each includes a section entitled Aspects, which explains the qualities associated with that direction. When we study movement on the Wheel in the chapter entitled Spiraling to the Center, you will find a chart in which all of these aspects are summarized.

Preparing for the Journey

Just as you would arrange carefully for any pilgrimage or sacred journey, you will ready yourself in specific ways to embark on the Path of the White Wolf. At the back of the book, in the section called Resources, you will find everything you need to gather for the journey, including basic tools, as well as instructions for practices and ceremonies and explanations for key concepts. You will refer to this section for clarification and support to prepare for each meditation and ceremony.

A foundational tool of this coursework is meditation. The meditations in each chapter, also available on the Path of the White Wolf meditation CD, are vehicles for profound inner discovery and growth. The drumming accompaniment for the meditations is also noted in the text.

As you move through the meditations from chapter to chapter, your understanding will open up and you will begin to "know that you know." The experiential format of each chapter supports personal discovery of each teaching's Medicine or essence, without extensive influence from others' experiences. You may find yourself gradually realizing just how familiar the Path of the White Wolf is to you.

Move at your own pace, as quickly or slowly as you like, spending as much time as you need to absorb each teaching. Feel free to creatively explore the meditations, written exercises, personal rituals, and questions presented in each chapter. We invite you to keep a dream journal to chronicle teachings received in the dreamtime.

There is no right or wrong way to use the concepts and tools in this book; what is most important is that you do the work. Each of us has a unique study style. Some study best solo; others learn best in a group (see Working in Community in the

Seven Sacred Directions

East – air, spring, yellow, dawn, awareness and illumination, eagle

South – fire, summer, red, day, trust and innocence, coyote

West – water, fall, black, dusk, introspection and dreaming, bear

North – stones, winter, white, night, ancestral wisdom and power, buffalo

Above – space, eternal, indigo, timeless, universal consciousness, star people

Below – organic, yearly, moss green, midnight, pregnancy of possibility, subterraneans

Center – magic, now, rainbow, dreamtime, integrated connection, Those Who Come and Go (guides and helpers)

Resources section). Each chapter includes suggestions and guidelines for group and interactive discussion. You can select the best study method for your learning style, or employ a combination.

To delve deeply into the Medicine of each teaching, we suggest that you spend a month on each chapter. When the lessons are completed consecutively, the course is a nine-month process that culminates in the completion ceremony in the final chapter.

The Medicine Wheel

The Path of the White Wolf spirals around the Medicine Wheel, which represents the Wheel of life. The Medicine Wheel encompasses all that is, and symbolizes the interconnection of all things. Ancient Medicine Wheels—great circles of stone placed by native peoples eons ago on sacred ground—exist in the United States and Canada, in South America and Europe, and in other places around the world. Medicine Wheels empower ceremony and ritual. Our forefathers and mothers knew by experience the Medicine Wheel's great power to initiate change and healing.

Often, these stone circles are aligned with landmarks to designate yearly cycles such as solstices, equinoxes, and astrological events. The Medicine Wheel aspects and concepts presented in this book help us view patterns and relationships, understand natural life cycles, and orient ourselves as we spiral through experience.

The Medicine Wheel we use in the Path of the White Wolf has four outer quadrants representing the cardinal directions: East, South, West, and North; and three center or inner directions: Above/Sky, Below/Earth, and Center/Within. These inner directions, along with cross-directional lines that link directions, expand the Wheel into three dimensions.

The cross-directional line that links the East/West directions signifies the joining of spirit and matter, and is the Blue Road of spiritual attainment. The line that delineates the marriage of North and South symbolizes the union of creativity and wisdom,

Sacred Seven

The sacred number seven, the number of personal transformation, signifies contemplation, analysis, a search for personal truth and spiritual understanding, and completion gained from true insight. Ancient religions contain many references to Sacred Seven: seven sacraments, seven virtues, seven sins, seven petitions, seven ceremonies, seven gifts of the spirit—implying that once you attain the seven, you are indeed complete, transformed. As humans our energetic fields resonate with the energies of the seven chakras.

The number seven, like the wolf, is associated with the moon, suggesting reflection (sunlight reflected from the moon) and introspection, intuition, and mystical spirituality. We live within the construct of a seven-day week, with the seventh day being a day of rest. As we rest at the number seven, we pause and take stock, understand where we stand and how we stand, and identify what we've learned, in order complete the cycle and step again on the path.

The number seven also relates to the law of octaves. The ancients knew and understood this law of the vibrations of sound and color, which emit wavelength vibrations of varying sizes that determine tone or hue. The law of octaves, as it applies to musical sound, is the use of seven sounds, repeating again at the first tone one octave higher, or seven notes with the eighth note repeating the tone of the first note, one generation above.

There are also seven hues, sometimes eight, visible in the rainbow: red, orange, yellow, green, blue, indigo, and violet. (Magenta is the eighth color and the hardest to see.) The same colors, usually invisible to the naked eye, are a part of the human aura, which can now be photographed through a process called Kirlian photography.

and is the Red Road of the physical plane. The connecting line from the Above/Sky Direction to the Below/Earth Direction grounds inspiration, linking Universal Consciousness to the earth plane of existence and uniting purpose with passion. Together, the teachings of the Circle along with its intersecting crosses create a framework for the integration and diversity of the universe itself.

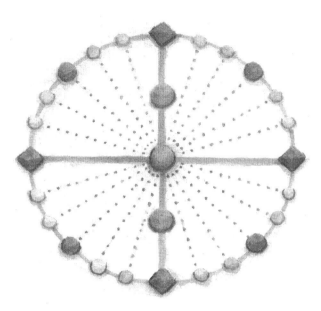

To take this image one step further, if we visualize the cross-directional lines as infinity symbols or figure eights, with all three infinity symbols linked together in a firmly held core, the Wheel's image is that of a multidimensional flower—ever-expanding, growing, blooming. When we sit at the center of the Wheel and view the image holographically, we *are* the connecting center, which allows us to speak of the Center direction.

As you consider this multidimensional image or spherical construct, you will see how changes in one part effect changes in another. Similarly, the changes in yourself as you use these teachings will affect your relationships at home, at work, in your community, and throughout the world. Like ripples caused by a stone falling into a pond, waves of transformation will spread out into the world as you change.

The Medicine Wheel colors and attributes we present here originate primarily with the Okanagon peoples. Much of the information on aspects and qualities is derived from other Native American teachings. The Path of White Wolf integrates practices taught in Asia, Africa and Europe, Siberia and Australia, and the teachings of the Mayan and Inca peoples of South America. In this way, we offer a Universal Medicine Wheel and a comprehensive set of instructions for use in the twenty-first century.

Our intention is to meld the best of past and present to form a full-spectrum learning cycle. The path around the Medicine Wheel is an ancient circular one, with bisecting lines North to South and East to West that have been added to reflect the modern, linear approach to teaching and learning.

We approach teaching with the view that each of us is born with basic characteristics that resonate with the perceptions and abilities inherent in the elements, the season, the attributes, and the totemic clan animal(s) of a particular quadrant. The Medicine Wheel introduced here is an Earth-based system that takes us *within ourselves* to find knowledge and answers to dilemmas, whereas sun-based, astrological systems guide us in understanding influential forces *outside ourselves.*

As your study of Medicine Wheel teachings broadens, you'll find that different tribes associate different aspects or teachings with the various directions. For instance, on White Wolf's path the element of Air, one of the Four Winds of Powers, is in the East. Some teachers put Fire in the East, which moves other directional aspects one quarter of the way around the Wheel. This adjustment presents a different perspective of the Wheel, and neither is more or less correct—it's simply a matter of your tradition.

Although there are many paths and many beginnings, on the Spiral Path you always begin again in the East, the place of all beginning. Your individual evolutionary path determines what you will perceive and manifest, and what will remain in the realms of the undetectable and invisible. The spiral teaching embodies the universal axiom: as within, so without. You follow the winding road around the Wheel, moving above, below, and within. As you complete the cycle, you move out again to the beginning position, to a new and higher evolutionary education—your next series of lessons.

Keys to Initiating Life Pattern Changes

Wise ones in many traditions tell us that the only constant is change. Well, change may very well be constant, but what about that old axiom "the more things change, the more they stay the same"? Which is it—each day a new dawn, or nothing new under the sun?

For millennia, spiritual seekers have endeavored to learn and change quicker, better, faster, to obtain knowledge and enlightenment, to truly understand the world. And the question remains: How do we get there from here?

There are two ways to initiate life pattern changes: intensity and repetition.

Intense experiences leave you forever changed. There is no returning from the point of transformation. The healing or scars you acquire may be with you always in this lifetime, and you may carry them forward into others.

Repetition, on the other hand, requires commitment, and you may encounter some resistance. Your ego, speaking to you through your mind, will not want to change and will balk at the repetition required to initiate change. If you choose the path of repetition, when you become aware of this resistance, ask yourself who's in charge . . . you or your ego? Your ego will want to stay in control, comfortable with what's familiar—whether it works or not.

At the same time, you may be holding on to old beliefs that no longer serve you. Remember, your subconscious cannot always distinguish current from past reality, or from illusion. Some core beliefs were programmed long ago, and it will take effort, time, and repetition to disengage them. It takes 21 days to learn something new and initiate change all the way to your core beliefs and subconscious; it takes 5,000 repetitions to make something second nature.

The lessons on the Path of the White Wolf work on the mental, physical/cellular, emotional, and spiritual levels. Many memories, especially traumas, are stored at the cellular level. The limiting beliefs and fears we carry as a result of these traumas affect our present reality. On this journey, you will work to physically release these limitations. Through all the practices we offer here, including sound, movement, and meditation, your energy will be freed and flow through your senses—your eyes, ears, taste, and feelings—and you will transform.

The Nature of Beginnings

And so you meet White Wolf at the beginning, to take your first steps on the path, knowing that as one of Mother Earth's children you must continue to evolve. Many of us feel sadness in our hearts that because of human "intelligence," Western culture has lost much. Business and industry continue to develop technologies without having the foresight or planning to assess the consequences and the effects on all Earth's inhabitants; the imbalances caused by pollution, over-population, war, greed, and dissatisfaction abound on our lovely planet, breaking natural law. Some of us can almost remember a time when human beings knew their oneness with all of creation, when none of Earth's families were placed above or below any other; a time when humans respected all beings—plant, animal, mineral, swimmers or flyers, walkers or crawlers—and their unique gifts. For those of us who recognize the disparity between exploiting our Earth Mother and developing lifeways to walk in balance with All Our Relations, it is time to find our way home.

Process of Manifestation

- **Inspiration** – When ideas come into your consciousness.
- **Intention** – Identifying and clarifying your vision or desire.
- **Calling** – Visualization or guided meditation to open to possibility and to additional information from Spirit.
- **Passionate purpose** – Connecting with your heart's desire, integrity, and caring.
- **Disciplined application** – Exploring deeper by asking questions, observing your world, making a commitment to the work.
- **Creation** – Working to birth your desires in the world.
- **Initiation** – The first physical manifestation. Your own experience combined with your personal understanding of your creation.

Path of the White Wolf

The Path of the White Wolf is a path of universal peace that begins with developing a relationship with yourself. You start by working on yourself to realize your individual potential and come into alignment with natural law. At the same time, you develop skills to help your brothers and sisters effect the same changes within themselves. As part of the consciousness that supports personal and global spiritual evolution, you walk gently upon the Earth as you play your part in realizing the dream of peace for all.

Yet as you explore your potential, you must own the fact that every day, in every moment you, as all humans, perform divine functions of creation and destruction. Our creations are rarely what we envision them to be. We imagine that we have the whole picture, but we don't. Our expectations both limit and sabotage us. As you travel the Path of White Wolf, you will open to the abundance of the universe and begin to trust that what the Creator—or Great Mystery—can add to your desires is good for all and bigger than anything you dare to imagine. The lessons on the Spiral Path will connect you more deeply to the Great Mystery, and move you beyond self-imposed limitations to embrace abundance.

The adventure you are about to begin offers you the priceless knowledge that you are an interconnected and interdependent student of the Great Mystery, and brother or sister to all Earth's children.

We offer this work out of respect, reverence, and love for All Our Relations.

Raptor Medicine

Eagle Spirit, Sky Raptor,
Filled with incredible Power,
Riding the thermal winds
In balance with Great Mystery,
Gathering your forces to plummet
To Earth to fill your needs,
Never taking more than what is yours,
Never wasting Mother Earth's abundance.

Teach me, Elder Brother
To claim my Power that I may
Soar the ether and float the warm winds
Of Father Sky's Grace
'Til I return to Earth's embrace,
To her gentle, welcoming womb,
To rest and sustenance once more,
Then to rise to fill my people's needs.

Hawk Woman, Snake Captor,
Who carries the Night Thief
In strong-as-iron talons,
I watched you carry him away,
Warrior of the Dawn,
Removing the threat to your young
With a mighty battle cry
That rends the morning mist.

Teach me, Proud Sister,
Your predator Medicine Song,
That I may capture and remove
The Thieves that slither through my soul,
The fear that steals my spirit song,
So that your Power within me
May unfold the wings of Hawk Medicine
To All My Relations.

Robin Tekwelus Youngblood

Aspects of the East

Element: *Air*
Embodiment: *Spiritual*
Emotions: *Awareness/Excitement*
Season: *Spring*
Time: *Dawn, Morning*
Moon Cycle: *Waxing*
Phase of Life: *Being Without Form*
Color: *Yellow*
Creatures: *Winged Ones*
Expression: *Voice, Flute, Instruments using Breath*
Way: *Seeker of Vision*
Place on the Wheel: *New Beginnings and Inspiration*
Lesson: *Awareness and Illumination*
Ceremony: *Calling Home*

*Starting
in the*
East

We enter the Medicine Wheel in the East, where spirit enters, at the doorway to the Wheel. The East signifies the place before birth and of birth, where we begin anew, over and over again. While standing at the East gate of the Medicine Wheel in our spirit form, we make the choices that determine our path in this life. We choose the destiny we wish to fulfill. Our choices determine the family into which we will be born and the life experiences we draw to ourselves.

When you find yourself in the East, you can be sure that something has ended and that you stand on the doorstep of a new beginning (whether you want to be there or not). It is time to identify, illuminate, and clarify, to seek vision and inspiration, to locate your new path and choose your new form. Each time you need to understand a situation in your life, you will return to the East, the place of initial choice, to accept what you chose when you entered this lifetime.

In the East you are the Seeker of Vision and welcome new ways of seeing. You pay attention to the world with fresh eyes as you develop new perspectives and find inspiration for each cycle of learning. New perspective enables you to experience the East's lessons of awareness and illumination.

Working in the East entails viewing life events in a different light and seeing what was shrouded in darkness. You may not understand what is illuminated, but at least you can see it—it is no longer hidden. With growing awareness—even though it may be an awareness of your lack of awareness—you acknowledge the importance of being fully present. You begin to pay attention, pay attention, pay attention to everything in your environment. You rely on physical and intuitive senses by relaxing your eyes and taking in a wider vista. You will notice things that escaped your attention or were previously hidden.

The East is the place of the rising sun, of new awakenings and dawning awareness. As the fog of night clears, you can see in a single moment the elements of your entire lifespan. You can see a new cycle beginning. What excitement awaits you! The moon cycle is waxing, growing into fullness, balancing light and darkness.

East is associated with spring, dawn, and morning. Its color is yellow; its element is air or wind. It is home of the winged ones. Eagle and hawk, with their high, spiraling flight and keen eyesight, are of the East. We see deer, weasels, and other animals here, but the winged ones embody the East's primary quality of air and the soaring flight of dawning awareness.

The song of the East rings through the air as purity of voice, the free-flowing sound of flute and other breath instruments. In your work with the East, you may hear a song without words or a chant with sounds like *hey, oh, ah, ya, an, ha*. Remember these sacred sounds. Sing them! You may find your song here.

Welcome to this journey, to this place of beginning on the Wheel. Welcome to the East, to the teachings of eagle and the essence of wind. Welcome to vision, illumination, and greater awareness, as the Wheel turns in this spiral of learning.

Aho!

Vision Quest

Throughout history, civilizations have recorded the visions of people gifted with extraordinary sight. Sacred books such as the Bible, the Koran, the Torah, and the scriptures of Hinduism and Buddhism tell us that visionaries hold a special place in all cultures, for they see what no one else can. Each Native American tribe honors the stories of their people's visionaries. Some of the most famous visions include Black Elk's world peace and horse dance visions, Crazy Horse's battle-winning vision for the Little Big Horn, the Ghost Dance vision practiced by the Sioux in the 1890s which led to the massacre at Wounded Knee, and the vision that created the Five Civilized Tribes of the Iroquois Nation.

Many indigenous societies practice some form of Vision Quest, calling it by different names. The Australian Aborigines, for example, embark on the Walk About. In the Native American tradition, those who seek vision for themselves practice *hanblecya* (crying for a vision) by removing themselves from the day-to-day world in order to experience inspiration, gain awareness, and receive direction from spirit. Young tribal members embark on Vision Quest at puberty to find their life purpose and guardian spirit power. Each seeker ventures into the wild to find an isolated place where he builds an altar. There he fasts and prays to the ancestors and powers of the seven directions for two to four days. At the end of this period, he returns from the quest with gifts from spirit that empower him to walk forward into the future.

In our society, we rarely make space to be alone with nothing but our thoughts for any length of time, let alone for several days in nature. Some of us make sure that we don't have any time to be alone because we fear what we will find if we look inside ourselves too deeply. And the thought of spending three or four days by ourselves in a natural environment can be terrifying. We imagine all the disasters that could happen—what if a wild animal devours us? Yet time alone in nature can heal and transform our lives.

Robin's most recent Vision Quest was on the island of Maui. Here she describes the profound effect of her quest.

I was in one of the few places in the world where my site faced a black sand beach and the ocean—in the South! South (trust) was my issue. I sat in a semicircle of ancient stone people with four grandmother faces in the rocks, and a sacred ceremonial cave a hundred feet from my site. The moon was full, the sun hot. One afternoon I was blessed with the sun setting to my right and the moon rising on my left with a rainbow around it. The next morning the sun rose on my left, the moon set on my right, and the rainbow followed the moon.

The air was full of magic. I sang, danced, and prayed; sat in silence and contemplation; felt the Earth beneath me, cradling me with gentle love; experienced the heat of the sun's fire, the whisper and roar of the wind on the water, and the tumble of stones rolling in the waves.

As always, my thoughts were very busy for the first two days, distracting me from my purpose. With a little practice, however, I was able to watch the thoughts flow by as a viewer watching a film—no attachment, no judgment, just perception and allowance. I had come to this quest to overcome fear and lack of trust in certain situations in my environment. I watched the fearful thoughts as they marched across the screen of my mind, and let them go one by one.

By the middle of the second day my mind quieted. I drifted with each moment, tasting and touching each sensation, marveling in simplicity. Each second became distinct and precious. I was once told that every grain of sand is a prayer that has been prayed at some time by someone. As I let a handful of sand sift through my fingers, I gave thanks for all our prayers.

A poem began to come, and then a song, "On the Wings of the Wind She Rides." I could see myself riding the skies like an eagle, in freedom and harmony with the universe and All My Relations. I experienced an in-flooding of peace, permeating my being and washing away the last vestiges of the fear I had carried. Along with it came a feeling of quiet joy that built to bursting point, until I had to dance and sing the Wheel of Life. While I didn't receive a visual symbol of my experience in this instance, my Vision Quest had been successful.

You may not have the time, support, or inclination to go on a Vision Quest or personal retreat, but the three-week written exercise in this section will help you identify your personal vision at this place on the Wheel.

A key to self-discovery on this path is reconnecting with the natural world, and throughout this year as you follow the Spiral Path of the White Wolf, you will experience nature in many ways. You will also become familiar with your inner landscape through the paradigm of the Medicine Wheel. You will sing, chant, and dance; you'll spend moments in utter stillness; you will dream and have visions. The teachings of White Wolf will help you to find deeper purpose and greater vision for your journey here on Earth.

You may want to wait until you complete one spiral of the Wheel before you pursue Vision Quest in nature. Many seekers take an entire year to prepare for Vision Quest, and only take the journey with the assistance of an experienced teacher. While some take the journey alone, we suggest that when you are ready you ask a Medicine Person to "put you on the hill." This person will pray with and for you, tend a sacred fire to enhance your strength and intention, and offer a Sweat Lodge for your purification. She will also help you to interpret the signs, dreams, visions, and encounters you experience on your quest.

Meditation of the East

Prior to beginning the meditation exercise, use the techniques described in Meditation: Basic Tools in the chapter entitled Preparing for Study, part of the Resources section at the end of the book.

Please remember throughout your journey that there is no right or wrong meditation experience. If it seems that nothing happened, wait and try again. Continue your practice day by day.

And now, meditation.

Visualize yourself in harmony with all creation, listen to the drum heartbeat of Mother Earth, and use your breath to sink deeper into relaxation and trance.

You find yourself standing in the trees at the edge of a small meadow. The sun has just risen and the sky is clear with a few clouds in the distance. The grass underfoot is new growth, bright clear green, undulating gently in the warm breeze. Flowers peek out from the grasses, raising their lovely faces to Father Sun. You might see other animals going about their business in or around the meadow.

You notice a rock a ways out into the meadow, and you walk out to it. You sit down and survey the beauty before you. You can smell the fragrance of moist earth, new growth, and pine, as the wind caresses your face and hair. There is still a hint of coolness in the air from the snow still on the distant mountains, but not enough to make you uncomfortable. You turn toward the east where the sun is cresting the treetops and shining on the meadow, where a few other rocks sit like sentries, watching and witnessing all that passes this way.

High in the sky flies Grandfather Eagle. You admire his effortless flight—the way he rides the wind and coasts, circling in warm thermals, rising higher and higher. He dives toward

Earth, and you notice his strength and beauty as he tucks his wings and cries out. You smile and thank spirit for this gift, offering a pinch of tobacco to the east.

You close your eyes for a few moments and feel the wind gently brush against you. Take a moment to experience this sensation—how it feels in your hair, through your fingers. Breathe deeply of its essence. After a few minutes you open your eyes to find yourself staring into the eyes of Eagle, perched on a rock opposite you. His eyes bore deep into you; you know he sees all that you are, but you are unafraid because you know he will not harm you.

In some inexplicable way you sense an invitation from him, and as you meet him to join in spirit, he takes to the air. You watch the ground beneath you fall away as you fly with him. Your body remains seated on the rock below, protected by the other stone sentries. You begin to experience the sensation and freedom of flight . . . how adjustments to certain feathers change speed and direction, how it feels to ride the wind.

You listen to the wind's song. You hear its voice, its timeless melodies rising in symphonic crescendo and fading to a whispering lull. This song speaks to you of all possibilities and the limitlessness we can claim if we would but just *see*.

As you soar higher and higher, you view the landscape of the Earth through eagle eyes. You see everything from a very great distance with remarkable clarity, yet you can focus on minute details if you choose. In the distance you see the mountains still capped with snow, and to the west a small lake glistening like a jewel.

Then you hear Eagle silently say to you, "Pay attention," and the landscape below fades into a spiraling timeline of your life. You see from high above the beginning of your earthwalk, your birth. Allow yourself to see, as a film running on a screen, the key events that formed each of your positive beliefs about yourself and the world in which you live. Relax and let the pictures flow through your mind. *(Beat the drum rhythmically for a minute or so.)*

Breathe deeply and feel the reassurance of Eagle in tune with the heartbeat of the universe. Hear the drum. Feel yourself connected to all that is, and look now at those events that formed each of your negative beliefs about yourself and your life, your character, your persona. Don't judge them—just see the pictures as they flow into and out of your mind. Try to associate each belief with its source. *(Drum for a few minutes.)* Ask Eagle for help with this, and note his perspective and how he illuminates these situations for you.

Relax and breathe deeply as Eagle brings you back to Earth, and you reenter your body that is still sitting on the rock in the meadow. Feel yourself grounded into yourself once more; you are no longer one with Eagle. You are back on Earth, and Eagle sits opposite you on one of the other rock sentries. You thank him for his gift by touching your fist to your heart, signifying that your heart is full and you are grateful. He looks at you one more time with intensity and understanding, then jumps to the air and leaves the meadow with stately grace and power.

You stand and begin to walk back toward the trees from where you first entered the meadow. As you reach the forest you place your hand on the first tree, and in that moment you begin to sink back to this time and place. *(Drumming changes to a different, faster beat for a minute or so to call the journeyer back.)* Enter your body in the here and now.

When you are ready, open your eyes. Write down all that you saw and thought, and begin to work on answering the questions in the next section.

Journal

1. After the meditation, use your journal to chronicle your journey with Eagle.

2. List the positive beliefs you discovered in this guided meditation. Identify what other strengths you bring to the table. Make a list and keep it in a place where you can review it during the month (at a different time of day than when you do your written exercise). Add to it as you discover more strengths and abilities.

3. List the negative beliefs you discovered on your journey, and note the source of each (perhaps Eagle gave you information during the meditation). Did you find you had any judgments about your negative beliefs? What were they, and did they follow a pattern?

4. Assess your goals for this year. Do they support all aspects of you: mental, physical, emotional, spiritual? How do they make use of your strengths? Do they challenge your weaknesses? How? Revise as needed.

5. In your journal, record dreams and other visions that you experience during this time. Identify how they supplement or clarify your work in the East.

6. Define your relationship to wind. What sensations or thoughts does wind bring to you? Describe the wind's song. Consider your relationship to your breath, and observe it coming in and going out. What do you notice?

7. Do you currently make room in your life to connect to vision? How and when? Do you invite vision and inspiration to assist you in finding answers to questions or predicaments?

The Ultimate Man or Woman

A Three-Week Written Practice

For the next three weeks—21 days—write for approximately 15 or 20 minutes per day. The effectiveness of this exercise depends on its being done every day, preferably at the same time each day. If you miss a day, start over at day one.

You'll be writing about "The Ultimate Man or Woman." This person is the most balanced, inspired, and enlightened person you can imagine. Begin each day's essay with the phrase "The Ultimate Man/Woman . . ." Describe the details of this person's life: where he or she goes, who he or she is in the community, where he or she lives. Describe how he or she looks: posture, manner of walking, sound of voice, style and color of clothes, etc. You've got 15 or 20 minutes a day—lots of time—to be descriptive. During the three weeks, explore every aspect of this person's life.

- Appearance
- Significant Relationships
- Family
- Job
- Daily Routine
- Activities
- Interests
- Living Environment and Location
- Spiritual Practices
- Vacations
- Possessions
- Talents and Abilities
- Anything and everything else you can think of

You'll find that your writing will go through stages, or a progression. Perhaps for a day or so you will write along the same thoughts or in the same form, and then another day it will seem radically different. Just keep going. This writing exercise is an important commitment and, in the end, you'll find it valuable.

Of course the process will bring up issues for you. Remember: what comes up is on its way out. Use your journal (or an alternative method that works for you, such as a tape recorder or art or dance) to process your thoughts and feelings, and to gain clarity and understanding.

At the end of the three weeks, you will begin to release what you no longer need in the manner that works best for you. (In the South you will perform the release again.) Use your completed "Ultimate Man or Woman" essay in the Calling Ceremony detailed below.

Calling Ceremony

For a list of tools and general setup instructions, see Basic Tools for Ceremony in the chapter entitled Preparing for Study, part of the Resources section at the end of the book.

- Locate a medium-sized clear quartz crystal that fits easily into your hand. Cleanse the crystal by soaking overnight in salt water.
- Choose a private indoor or outdoor site for your ceremony.
- Build a simple four-directions Medicine Wheel Circle, with one stone in each cardinal direction.
- Bring your drum or rattle.
- Put the environment in order and have your journal at hand.
- Set Sacred Space.
- Smudge for clearing and cleansing.
- Ground yourself, establishing your connection to the Earth.
- Review your Intention.
- Say a prayer for protection.
- Request the presence of guides and other helpers.
- Read "The Ultimate Man or Woman" essay aloud to yourself, and place it in the center of the Circle.

Stand facing the East at the east point of the Wheel. Call in the Great Eagle and all the Powers of Good in the East to the stone Circle, and ask them to help you become more fully the Ultimate Man or Woman you wrote about. Begin to sing to the Spirits of the East using your drum or rattle as accompaniment. You can sing songs that you know, or just allow your voice to create melodies with sounds or vocables like *oh* or *heya*. It doesn't matter if you think you sing well or not. Just allow yourself to express through your voice what you feel and experience. Experiment with singing, in words, a prayer to the Spirits of the East or Eagle. Let it rhyme if it wants to and allow your music and song to flow naturally. Ask spirit to give you words and phrases. Open to the *feeling* of Spirit Within.

When you have finished in the East, move to the South and call or sing in the Medicine of the South: trust, innocence, love, and joy. Repeat this in the West (introspection, dreaming, and balance) and North (wisdom, integrity and authenticity, leadership). Then ask Father Sky and Mother Earth to bless you abundantly in your quest to be your own Ultimate Woman or Man.

Now, at the point where you call in the center of the Wheel, take out the crystal. Sit near the center of the Circle next to your "Ultimate Man or Woman" essay, and hold the crystal in your left hand, your receiving hand. Relax and ground, feeling yourself and the crystal to be the center of the Medicine Wheel Circle.

Focusing on the crystal, send it the energy of your love. Do you feel a response? Crystals are record keepers and holders of wisdom. This crystal will work with you to hold the vision of your Ultimate Man or Woman. Ask the crystal to hold this vision for you.

Now visualize the person you described in your essay, and place this individual in the crystal. Close your eyes and send the images and pictures from your mind into the crystal. As you see this vision in your mind's eye, claim the image of this person as your vision of yourself. Take as long as you need to do this.

From now on, when you need this vision with you or wish to connect with this image, you can tap into the information/image stored in your crystal. If it is difficult to see yourself as the Ultimate Woman or Man, use the crystal in meditation—hold it in your hand or place it in your lap—to connect with your vision, with who you really are.

Now hold the crystal to your heart, and sit for awhile in the center of the Medicine Wheel. Let go of your thoughts and let them flow through your mind without paying attention to any of them. Visualize Grandfather Eagle sitting on his rock out in the meadow as you did in the meditation. Feel his eyes upon you and sense his keen awareness. Revisit the clarity and illumination he shared with you in meditation, and ask if he has any other messages for you as you complete the lessons of the East. Listen for his answer. When you are finished, open your eyes.

Close the Circle by releasing each direction in the reverse order that you called it in. Thank the spirits and guides for their support, including the spirits of the land where you spent this time. Leave the site more beautiful than when you found it by placing a small offering, a bundle of herbs, a flower, or a pinch of tobacco.

Butterfly Woman

In the shadowy flicker of candle flame
I see Butterfly Woman enter my dreams again.
This time her wings shine iridescent blue-black
With tiny sequins that reflect
Starlight from the fertile mystery of the
Crack between the worlds.

She sings with clear voice of
Transformation, of going within to
Emerge changed.
I continue to invite her into my life,
Although she is a challenging taskmaster with
Difficult lessons.

Aloft she presents a fiery crystal to
Grandmother moon and
Washes it in the ocean of the void to
Place on my forehead.
I dream that in each of her wing panels I see
Scenes of ancient people

> *Lighting candles . . . Tending children*
> *Finding stillness . . . Hunting deer*
> *Sewing clothing . . . Gathering herbs*
> *Planting crops . . . Chopping wood*
> *Seeking in themselves divinity, creativity,*
> *strength, compassion, hope*

I sleep fitfully for what seems an eternity,
Facing nightmares of my fearful selves.
I fall and rise with skinned knees and bleeding heart.
I cry until I can cry no more.
Finally, I awaken to bask in warm light.
Amazed, in different form, I spread my wings and fly.

Butterfly Woman winks at me in the mirror.
Why did I never notice her sitting on my shoulder?
Butterfly Woman smiles at me through the eyes of my
daughter.
Why did I never notice her within others?

Butterfly Woman dances in the void awaiting your call.
I am/you are/she is/we are Butterfly Woman.

Sandy D'Entremont

Element: *Fire*
Embodiment: *Physical*
Emotions: *Anger/Passion/Elation*
Season: *Summer*
Time: *Noonday*
Moon Cycle: *Full*
Phase of Life: *Young Adult*
Color: *Red*
Creatures: *Four-leggeds*
Expression: *Drum and Dance*
Way: *Creator of Movement*
Place on the Wheel: *Growth, Learning, Work with Joy*
Lesson: *Trust and Innocence*
Ceremony: *Dancing the Fire*

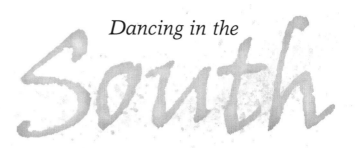

Dancing in the South

Fullness of summer, passion, and love of life reside in the South, the place of laughter, love, and learning on the physical plane.

Here on the Medicine Wheel you connect with the child within. Your eyes view the world with trust and innocence. Seeing in this way, you know that you are safe and that your needs are met. The world is a friendly place and nothing ill can befall you.

The South is the place of possibility and truth. You feel here great love toward all manner of things and perceive the beauty of the world. Your glass is always half full.

Although this viewpoint may seem unrealistic, please suspend your disbelief and trust that this perspective can be a true perspective. It is the natural viewpoint of the healthy, loved child, whose state we yearn for.

Here you can manifest your dreams and live an inspired life, for in the South resides the young adult, full of ideas, inspiration, and energy. The South is the place of full expression. Your connection with the impassioned fire of creativity compels you to dance to the drum on warm evenings and gaze at the fullness of the moon in the embrace of your lover. South is the element of fire, representing transformation, creativity, drive, and movement. You will find here, too, the angry fires of forbidden creativity flickering, searching longingly for release. You have the opportunity now to open the doors to your hidden artistry.

The color of the South is red, the color of blood and birth.

At this place on the Path of the White Wolf, your role is Creator of Movement and your objective is to birth your vision—to perform the labor of creation. This is a time of work, but also a time to enjoy the labor because you are in tune with your vision from the East. You will be working toward doing what you want to do, and as a result you will often experience great abundance (although your definition of abundance may change in the process).

In the South you will learn that you must balance work with play.

At this quadrant, you will incorporate the vision you found in the East with the trust you will practice in the South. Since you are now aware that you have a purpose to fulfill, it will be easier to trust that the support and encouragement you need to achieve it are available.

The four-leggeds reside here. Coyote and Mouse are most often associated with the South. Coyote, the trickster, shows you how to laugh at yourself—especially if you have forgotten how—and will not allow you to take life too seriously. Mouse is close to the ground, sees everything, misses nothing; she shows you how to take care of all the details, how to stay busy and focused on the task at hand. We see Beaver, the builder; Snake, the transmuter and protector; Rabbit, the fear-caller; and other creatures who have much to teach us here in the South.

The song of the South is the sound of the drum and the sound of your feet dancing in joy and celebration, a quick, rhythmic pounding that calls you to dance with abandon. This song can also be the quiet drumming of the Earth's heartbeat, which makes you know you've come home.

In the South you will find Heyokah or Contrary Medicine. The Heyokah are those whose vision impels them to see life in contrast to the majority. Heyokah people may seem backward; they may act or say the exact opposite of what they mean. Heyokah show us alternative perspectives, most often in a humorous manner—like the trickster Coyote—so we can cleanse ourselves with their medicine of laughter and learn something new. Do not be surprised if a Heyokah cries when everyone else is laughing. When you recognize a Heyokah, hold on to your hat and get ready to learn something!

Welcome to this journey, to this place on the Wheel. Welcome to the teaching of Mouse and Coyote and the essence of fire. Welcome to trust, innocence, and love, as the Wheel turns in this spiral of learning.

Aho!

When Rabbit Met Snake

This well-loved story is told in many cultures with different characters. It is best told aloud in a group, where you will see a childlike awareness in the eyes of your listeners.

It was a long time ago . . . a long, long time ago . . . I mean, a very long time ago. There was a little brown rabbit, the one they call Fear-Caller because he's so afraid of everything that he creates the very things he fears.

Well, Rabbit was searching for food, nice grasses and little berries on low bushes. Every few minutes he'd stop and sniff about him, scrunch down and cringe. Mostly he was afraid of Snake because everyone knows that snakes eat rabbits. Suddenly, sure enough, he heard the frightening takatakatakata of the rattlesnake. He plunged headlong into the nearest bush and cowered beneath it, shivering and sniffing for a whiff of scent. "Oh, no!" he thought. "My worst fears are realized. That snake is looking for me, and he's going to find me and eat me!"

Snake rattled again. Only this time, Rabbit thought he heard that the rattle was more like a painful thrashing. "Why," wondered Rabbit, whose second greatest quality was curiosity, "would a snake be in pain?" He was still crouched under the safety of the bush, but as Snake thrashed and rattled again, sounding weaker than before, Rabbit's curiosity got the better of him. He poked his

41

head out, sniffed carefully, and began to scan the hill below him.

Not so far away he saw an outcropping of stones. Beneath a large boulder he saw a shadow. And there was Snake, barely breathing, trying to move further under the rocks. Rabbit could see that Snake was terribly injured.

Summoning all his courage, Rabbit stepped out from beneath his bush. "Snake!" he called. "What's the matter?"

Snake looked up, angry and ashamed at being seen in such a helpless position. "Go away, Rabbit! Can't you see I'm trying to sleep?"

Rabbit thought, "A snake trying to sleep, exposed to the noonday sun? I don't think so! But what should I do?" His fear was almost overpowering, nearly immobilizing. Behind his thoughts a little voice kept repeating, "Watch out! Run away fool! Snakes eat rabbits!" But Rabbit knew Snake was badly hurt.

Tentatively, Rabbit hopped a little closer. "Snake, I can see that you're hurt. Truth is, I'm scared of you, but I can see you need help. If you promise not to eat me, I'll try to help you."

"You idiot!" shouted Snake, trying to maintain his arrogance. "Of course I'll eat you! That's what snakes do. SSSSSHHHHHH HSSSSTTT!!!" he screamed in sudden pain.

"I am hurt," Snake moaned in defeat. "If you help me, I promise I won't even try to eat you until I'm well again and we've gone our separate ways. After that, I can't make any guarantees—after all, I am a snake." He rattled his tail feebly.

Rabbit approached, still fearful but knowing he had to help. He simply couldn't stand by and see someone else—even a snake—in that kind of pain. (Another of Rabbit's lesser known qualities is loving empathy.) He saw that one of the coils on Snake's tail had a nasty cut. Knowing it was infected, he went about finding herbs and reeds to bind it. Rabbit's greatest fear was almost realized when he applied the poultice. In his pain, Snake forgot all his promises and lashed out, almost biting Rabbit in the neck.

Next the little hare went searching for food. Snakes are predators and rabbits aren't, so Rabbit wasn't sure how he was going to hunt for Snake. But down near the stream Rabbit found a dead mouse.

When he brought Snake the mouse, Snake's anger and sense
of self-importance melted. "Little friend, thank you," he said. "You
are helping me greatly. I don't even understand why you would do
this, since you know I could take your life any minute. I make you
a new promise. For your gift of healing, I will never hurt you or
your family."

Rabbit didn't really know what to make of Snake, or his prom-
ise. He saw that Snake feared his help almost as much as Rabbit
himself feared helping. And that was a new understanding. But
there would always be other snakes on other hillsides that would
gladly eat Rabbit for dinner.

Many animals sit at the South Gate of the Medicine Wheel.
Those you encounter depend on the lesson you are learning.
In this story, Rabbit sits in the South, the place on the Wheel
where you initially begin to surrender to your own processes,
and find the trust to do what must be done. When transformation
(Snake) knocks on your door, you may be afraid—will it take you
someplace you don't want to go? Will it harm you? What will you
have to give up to evolve into a new state of being? How much
work will it take? Like Snake in the story, we don't like to grieve
and hate the pain of loss that often accompanies transformation.
In our pride, it is so hard to admit that we hurt and even harder to
ask for help. Just as Rabbit cowered under the bush, we hide from
feelings to try to avoid consequences, mistakenly believing that if
we don't see it or talk about it, it isn't real.

Trust and fear are two sides of the same coin. Finding trust
and the courage to face your fears is a great challenge. Solace
comes in knowing that each surmounted fear heals you and
brings you a step closer to realizing your life's purpose. May we
all find a place of deeper connection to All Our Relations.

Meditation of the South

This meditation will guide you to your totem or power animal. Totem animals appear at different times for different reasons. The animal you find in this meditation may be one with which you already have, or will have, a long history; or it may be in your life for a short time for a specific reason. Don't over-analyze this in meditation. Just be open to what comes.

If you see many animals and are uncertain which to choose, the one who shows itself to you three times is the one for you, in this meditation. Remember that for this particular journey, your totem animal is not an insect, snake, creepy-crawler, or other fanged reptilian creature; if one of these creatures comes to you repeatedly, come out of the journey and try again another time.

Prior to beginning the meditation exercise, use the techniques described in Meditation: Basic Tools in the chapter entitled Preparing for Study, part of the Resources section at the end of the book.

Visualize yourself in harmony with all creation, listen to the drum heartbeat of Mother Earth, and use your breath to sink deeper into relaxation and trance.

Breathe light into your body, beginning at your feet and traveling upward toward your head. Consciously relax a particular part of your body with each breath. Draw the energy of Mother Earth, colored a velvety moss green, up through your feet to your pelvis, up into your solar plexus, heart, throat, third eye, and out through the crown of your head. Feel yourself letting go of all judgment. Become a willing observer.

You find yourself walking in bright sunshine along the top of a smooth rock ridge in the high desert. Below are rolling hills of granite and brush. The weathered rock tells the story of wind and water—a land that has seen much change over

millions of years. Under a clear sky the cliffs reflect many colors: rust-red, yellow-gold, gray, and white-green where lichen grows.

The places where the rock has turned to soil yield low grasses and other flowering plants, along with gray-green sage and bitterbrush bushes. Trees are but few here—only cottonwood in places where water settles or pines who seem able to gain purchase out of the very rock itself. You smell the unmistakable scent of sage as the breeze rises from the hills below.

As you continue along the hilltop you realize that there are many animals here. Swallows nesting in the cliffs circle above. Rabbit hops between the shady patches of sagebrush on the way to feed her young. You notice where marmots sit to survey the landscape below and the broken rock outcroppings where snakes escape the heat of day.

As you descend into a small saddle between hills, you notice a diverging trail that heads south toward the valley floor. Tracks on the trail tell you Coyote headed that way not long ago. You take the path and follow it between two hills, down a gentle grassy slope. The trail meanders between sage and bitterbrush, and cuts to the right into a canyon you had not seen before. You decide to walk a little further and explore the small sage-filled canyon hidden between granite cliffs.

You hike to the end of the canyon, and to your surprise find a small pool nestled between sage, boulders, and cliffs. One cliff side shows evidence of where water falls from high above during the rainy season, and the cliff is dark beneath in shade. You sit at the edge of the pool on one of the flat table-size stones that border one side. You close your eyes and relax into the beauty and peacefulness of this place, and the love you can feel from the Earth Mother. You are safe here. Give to yourself all the unconditional love you would give to a tiny child. Picture yourself as a small child, and begin to see and listen to the source or sources of your limiting beliefs—those that hold you back from being who you know you are. See this information through the eyes of yourself as a child.

Breathe deeply and feel the reassurance of the rock beneath, in tune with the heartbeat of the universe. Hear the drum, and feel yourself connected to all that is. Take this exercise slowly, remembering that you are only an observer. The South is the place on the Wheel of Life that expresses the purity and trust of a child. Remember that we are all children, acting in the innocence of each moment. This will enable you to release any self-judgment. *[Drum for a minute or so.]* Continue to breathe deeply.

Open your eyes, and drink in the clearness of the sky and the stillness of the pool. As you survey your surroundings once again and your eyes scan the perimeter of the pool, you find yourself looking into the eyes of a young coyote. He has been watching you for quite awhile from his comfortable hiding place under a bitterbrush bush where he has been chewing a bone. He shows no sign of alarm at your presence, but rises and stretches, yawning. He looks at you as if to say, "Ready?" and heads around the pool toward the cliff at the back.

He jumps onto a boulder, bounds to another, and then finally lands on a stone bench directly under the waterfall cliff. He looks back over his shoulder as if to say, "Coming?" and seems to be daring you to do so with a sarcastic grin. It is then that you notice the entrance to a cave in the shade of the cliff. You are initially uncertain about what to do, but your childlike sense of adventure, curiosity, and innate trust persuade you to go along.

You follow him, jumping boulder to boulder, and he leads you into the cave. . . . But it's not a cave, it's a tunnel, and once you enter you can see through it to fields on the other side. Shortly you are through and stepping into the high grasses with Coyote at your side. There is something very different about this landscape, but you keep going, letting Coyote guide your way onto the plains.

You begin to see many animals here. They seem quite friendly and may come up to you. Some may seem familiar, but you are looking for a certain one. When one particular animal comes to you more than once and shows itself to you from both sides, you'll know that this is the one for whom you came.

Hold out your hands to your totem animal and receive the magic of his or her essence. Invite this animal to become part of your life and to visit you in the dreamtime. *(Drumming a minute or so.)* Ask for the spirit of this animal to return with you, and go back to the tunnel entrance. Coyote will show you the way.

Come back through the tunnel and return to the rock at the pool's edge. Sit down again and take a deep breath. Thank Coyote for his guidance, and watch as he pads his way back down the trail. You cannot help but laugh as he looks back at you one more time with his tongue lolling out, smiling.

As you close your eyes in the sunshine by the edge of the pool, you begin to sink back to this time and place. *(Drumming changes to a different, faster beat for about a minute to call the journeyer back.)*

Enter your body in the here and now. When you are ready, open your eyes. Hold your hands to your heart and let the essence of your totem animal merge with your being. Write down all that you saw and thought, and begin to work on answering the questions below.

Journal

1. Use your journal to chronicle your high desert adventure.

2. Define the different types of love you have experienced in your lifetime, including when you had these experiences. How did it feel to love yourself unconditionally during the visualization?

3. Identify the sources of some of your limiting beliefs as seen through the eyes of the child within. Do the sources of these beliefs seem similar in some cases? Can they be grouped into categories?

4. Are any of the sources in Question 3 still present in your life? Do they still affect you in some way? How? What would it be like to detach from feeling any effects in your present life from these sources? Will there be consequences if you do this, and what might they be? Are you ready to do this?

5. Describe your totem animal. Research this animal: what are its habitats, habits, strengths, patterns? What does this animal mean to you? Is it predator or prey? If possible, acquire or create a representation of this animal for your altar.

6. Use your journal to record dreams and other visions experienced during this time. Identify how these supplement or clarify your work in the South.

7. Define what criteria are required for you to think of a particular activity as play, and contrast that with the criteria for a work activity. What key factors differentiate the two?

Imagination

This exercise involves three parts, each of which you will address over the next 21 days. To help you maintain the discipline of this exercise, invite White Wolf to be your witness.

Part One consists of creating a collage, a physical reflection of your completed goals and the life described in your Ultimate Man/Woman exercise. You'll need a poster board and glue, along with magazines, photographs, drawings, etc. from which you'll cut words and pictures. This exercise does not require an advanced art degree; it only requires your attention and intention as you collect the images and concepts. Include the following key elements:

- A representation of the Creator, the infinite, the Great Mystery or whatever represents the Divine source to you
- A picture of yourself in a happy situation or doing something that mirrors your goals
- Gratitude, whether the words "Thank You" or something similar
- A representation of your totem animal
- An image or word that reflects the concept of harmony, a reminder that these goals will manifest easily for the good of All Our Relations

Remember, this collage represents your heart's desire, the vision you hold. Don't include unwanted or negative images or words. Consider the elements of work and play as you envision your project, and allow the child within to have fun. When you are ready to assemble the collage, do so in an intentional, ceremonial way. See Basic Tools for Ceremony in the chapter entitled Preparing for Study, part of the Resources section at the end of the book. When the piece is completed, place it somewhere where you can see it every day.

In Part Two, you will carefully make note of your thoughts and feelings during this process. Do not be surprised if you can't seem to find anything "right" for the project, or alternatively feel overwhelmed by all the images that seem to "speak" to you, causing you to lose focus and become frustrated. As you collect images and words, your goals become clearer in your imagination. This is a powerful step in the manifestation process and it may bring up some old limiting thoughts. Write these thoughts down and examine them to see if they fit your current world view. Save for release in the integration ceremony.

Remember that the stuff that comes up is on its way out; use your journal to record these processes and feelings so that you can consciously release what you no longer need. Do this daily after you complete the exercise described in part one. You will use what you have written during the integration ceremony later.

In Part Three, you will divide your daily activities into Work and Play, and identify what you enjoy or love and dislike about each. You can do this as a chart, as illustrated below.

Note how your responses change over the three weeks. Where and why are there imbalances? How does this information fit with your vision of who you are and what you want to create? What is the message here for you?

When you complete this, move on to the integration ceremony.

Activity	Work, Play, Both	Enjoy/Love	Dislike
Customer service work	Work	Resolve Smith account	Customers
Dishes	Both	Working w/Jan	Dishpan hands
Walking the dog	Play	Running together	Barking dogs

Dance Ceremony

Now through dance you will integrate and express the energy and knowledge that you have gained. For a list of tools and general setup instructions, see Basic Tools for Ceremony in the chapter entitled Preparing for Study, part of the Resources section at the end of the book.

Circle the Wheel once, calling in the Powers of the Seven Directions with your drum, then enter at the gateway of the South.

Standing in the South, begin playing your choice of drumming music and call in Coyote. Bring his essence into your body and let it flow through you into dance, movement, and sound. Express playfulness, like a child, imagining yourself to be open and trusting. Don't worry about how you may appear to others. Allow yourself to growl and howl, roll on the ground and scratch your back! Have fun being Coyote. When you feel you have experienced Coyote to his fullest, kneel on the ground with your face down against the Earth. Release Coyote to the Mother.

Now call in your personal power animal. Feel this animal's energy enter your body. Rise and dance this essence, using movements you associate with this creature. As you pass through each quadrant of the Wheel, dance your animal as the Power of that Direction: Vision in the East, Trust and Love in the South, Introspective Dreaming in the West, and Powerful Wisdom in the North. Call forth the sounds that emanate from the Source of All Power within yourself, from all the primeval lineages you embody. *Be wild!* This is not about how others see you but what you find in the deepest regions of your self. Trust in yourself and in the safety of the universe, understanding that wildness and wilderness are natural states.

When you finish dancing the Wheel, release your power animal in the same way that you released Coyote. Thank both animals for joining you and helping you to feel their joy and freedom.

Now stand once again in the South and call in the Power of Fire. See it in your mind burning away that which no longer serves you. Take what you have written and the chart you made during your three-week exercise and read it, releasing to the fire all that caused you stress and negativity. If it is safe to do so, burn your writings and the chart in a fireproof bowl (or burn later, as appropriate). You no longer need to carry emotions that you do not want. Let them go, and be transformed.

When you complete this part of the ceremony, offer a pinch of tobacco, cedar, or sage to the ancestors at each gateway of the Medicine Wheel, and thank them for their watchful observance. They have witnessed all that you have done. Acknowledge their help from the Other World, and ask them to bless your work. Let the tobacco go to the ground or into the wind, if outdoors. If indoors, burn the tobacco in the fireproof bowl.

Close the Circle by releasing each direction you called, in reverse order. Thank the spirits and guides for their support, including the spirits of the land where you spent this time. Leave the site more beautiful than when you found it by placing a small offering, a bundle of herbs, a flower, or a pinch of tobacco.

In Lakesh

My love is a pillar of light
His eyes smoky crystalline pools
Radiant with love,
He sees with the vision of the eagle,
His scent is the musk of hibiscus,
He is strong as the gentle ocean.

Together my love and I danced the stars
Turning cartwheels in the night sky.
We spun the web of the universe,
Gossamer light trailed from our touch.

My heart soars with love for him
My soul is awe-inspired,
I open to him as a flower
Petal by soft shimmering petal.

He is wise with the knowledge
Of the ancient ones,
Pure as a newborn child.
His beauty is unsurpassed
And reflected in the many eyes
That look upon him.

He teaches me with each caress,
I bask in the warmth of his honor.
By acknowledging me so deeply
I become ever more fully myself.

My love is "In Lakesh"—
Another
myself
Purest reflection of all
God/Goddess within.

We stand in the Garden
Consummate in our creation
And we are one.
Our love-making waters the Earth,
Our joy transforms the universe,
The heavens explode with our love.
I meet my love
With all that I am
And all that I have to give,
That together we might serve.

This lover of mine
Is free as the rolling wave.
And I, I am
The wind on the water.

Many times have his house
And mine been joined.
We have traveled many
Worlds together.
Where we walk on the path
Wildflowers bloom.

Will I see his face again
In this lifetime?
My heart awaits his call,
Yet always we are one.

For my love is In Lakesh
Forever a part of me.
His presence lives within me,
His light which is mine
shines purely.

Robin Tekwelus Youngblood

Element: *Water*
Embodiment: *Fluidity/Emotion*
Emotions: *Grief/Joy*
Season: *Autumn*
Time: *Dusk*
Moon Cycle: *Waning*
Phase of Life: *Mature Adult*
Color: *Black*
Creatures: *Swimming Ones*
Expression: *Flowing Water or
    Waves Against the Shore/Silence*
Way: *Mirror*
Place on the Wheel: *Fluid Balance*
Lesson: *Introspection and Dreaming*
Ceremony: *Cleansing*

Cleansing in the *West*

West is the place on the Wheel where autumn and dusk reside, and where you reap what you have sown, for good or ill.

As you move into the West you bring all that you have learned in the East and South, a Medicine Bundle filled with your dreams and vision, and the playful, creative innocence of a trusting child. These ingredients will help you to heal. In order to know the light, you must face your own reflection through the process of introspection; within this reflection, you find both light and darkness: your own inner darkness. Remember that on this path White Wolf is with you and there is nothing to fear.

West is associated with water, the oceans and rivers, streams and lakes. Water nourished us in the womb and our bodies are composed primarily of water; water covers most of our planet. Life as we know it depends upon water, the primal and primary element.

Water is female and related to emotion. In this phase of your journey, you may be in close touch with your emotions and find that some of your internal struggles are being worked out in your dreams.

In the West reside the swimming ones. We find Salmon, who circles the oceans of the world in community and returns again to his place of birth in sacrifice for the next generation. Bear is associated with the West for being protective of her young, for her gift of dreaming, and for her annual and long turning within—hibernation—to begin the cycle again. We see Dolphin, Seal, Otter, and other animals in the West as well.

The sound of the West is the entrancing sound of flowing water and waves against the shore—sounds that can reveal the veil between the worlds. This veil is thinnest in the West. You are able to connect most easily with your guides and spirit helpers in the West by becoming silent and still in meditation, and by paying attention to your dream world.

In the West you discover your power of introspection. You look within yourself as a mature adult to assess who you are, where you've come from, and the choices you've made. West is the place where you can go under the surface to get in touch with the still, small voice within. Here you can mourn your losses and release the past once again, letting that which needs to die do so. Here you can witness your rebirth with joy.

As you work in the West, you begin to see the ebb and flow of your life, and the patterns and internal and external rhythms that help you embody the Medicine of flowing water, finding the path of least resistance. You can recognize and accept the male and female energies within you, and bring both together in a fluid symmetry. You can begin to feel more whole and balanced, less needy for someone else to provide you with this energetic balance.

When you arrive in the West, your task is to look closely into the waters of your own soul, into the mirror. Really look, with as little judgment as possible. You will see what you will see, including those characteristics, attachments, baggage, relationships, and traits that impede your growth. This process can be difficult. You can either emerge from these waters washed clean and reborn, or feel as though you are drowning in your own emotional stew.

Know that you create your own reflection. Your environment (physical reality) mirrors back to you who you are. In essence, your reality is only a mirror in which to see yourself more clearly. Understand that you create your own reality. You are responsible for where you are and who you are. Just as important, know that you can change your reflection by changing your perspective with this work.

So, what do you do if you don't like what you see in your mirror? Work on changing the mirror. When you change, the mirror will change. It's as simple as that. Mirroring works in relation to all aspects of your life, including other people. When you change, others (the mirrors) will change, or they will leave your life. As the saying goes—*as within, so without*. Recognize that you are a mirror for others as well.

Mirroring is a difficult concept to accept because it implies responsibility. But once you do accept it and realize its truth, you can empower yourself to create a new vision—you can paint a brand new reflection. Your artistry develops as you let go of your attachments and emotional baggage, and respond differently to situations and people in your life. New experiences and fresh approaches are born out of mindfulness, compassion, and forgiveness rather than the limitations of the past. Your new flexibility and balance allow you to move forward in a new way—and to see a new reflection.

Welcome to this journey, to this place on the Wheel. Welcome to the teaching of bear dreaming, salmon returning home, and the essence of flowing water. Welcome to introspection, reflection, and balance, as the Wheel turns in this spiral of learning. *Aho!*

Seal People

Many northern cultures tell stories of seals who transform themselves into human beings for a time, moving from sea to land, from this world to the other world. This movement between the realms of water and land is a return to the waters of birth and beginnings. Seal people guide us to a forgotten part of ourselves—often represented in story as a spouse—and to the watery realm of emotions and tides. In this return we find a homecoming, a healing, as is illustrated in this Inuit story.

Late into the dusk a man was hunting on the sea in his kayak. Hearing singing in the distance, he paddled to a little-known island and saw a group of naked women dancing with the moon. At the edge of the shore he saw the women's cloaks and he stole one of them, placing it in his kayak. When the women finished dancing they came to the shore and slipped on their cloaks, which were sealskins. The seals returned to the sea. The woman whose garment he held came to him looking for her skin cloak. Struck by her beauty he asked her to marry him, promising he would return her cloak in seven years. She did not want to stay with him but reluctantly agreed, and in time they had a beautiful son.

Over the years the dual challenges of living on land and being married to the hunter began to change the woman. Her beauty faded and her skin shriveled into wrinkles. Her legs weakened and she limped painfully. At the end of seven years she knew she had to return to her home in the ocean waters, or she would undoubtedly die. Although her love for her son was strong, the call of the sea was stronger. She cried and asked for her skin cloak back but the hunter refused, berating her for wanting to leave him.

One day as she was looking for some dried fish and moving some of their possessions from one place to another in their hut, she came across a basket she had never seen before. Inside was her skin, and she did not hesitate to wrap herself in the soft folds and revel in the feeling of home. She quickly left the hut and made her way to the ocean shore, stopping only to bid her son a tearful goodbye and assure him that she would continue to care for him.

As she sank under the waves, the sea lovingly embraced her. She was never seen again.

The son of the seal woman grew to manhood, and he always had the odd, persistent habit of fishing alone. No one knew where he went, but his catch was always abundant. Once on a foggy spring morning, some hunters thought they saw him sitting on the rocky point of a little-known island speaking to a seal, but the fog was unusually thick and none were certain that it was really him.

In our own dreams we often return, like the seal woman, to the other world, to depths of our soul. When you dream that you are underwater in another world, perhaps even able to breathe underwater, your journey is to find out something about your instinctual nature. These day- or night-dreams can illuminate hidden parts of you that need healing, and show you who you really are and what you want.

When you work with the Medicine of the West, pay close attention to your dreams. Dreamtime is a facet of reality. Problems or issues that need resolution in your waking reality find their way into your dreams. The insights you receive are important; you may wish to record them in your journal. In time you may find you are able to consciously affect the events in your dreams.

The dream story that follows was given to Sandy at a time when she needed to decide what course of study to pursue.

I was resting on my back in the water looking toward the shore of a tropical island. Beside me swam an otter, whom I recognized as my companion and friend. I think I was an otter, too. I was at home in the water, not cold or warm, not struggling to stay afloat. I could dive underneath the waves with my friend and see brightly colored fish and the coral reef. I knew we were supposed to go to the island and so we did, stepping onto the sandy shore in bright sunlight. The island seemed deserted.

A path through the trees led up toward the island's forested peaks. We climbed together, leaping over rocks and drinking from cool waterfalls. I came to a wide plateau where a community lived. Many members gathered in the town square for morning tai-chi. I joined them and spoke to the instructor after the session. We had tea together, and she told me she knew why I'd come. Would I come with her to the top of the mountain?

She and I hiked up the mountain into the clouds, coming at last to a Circle of upright, volcanic stones. We stood in the center of the Circle and felt the strong, calming Earth energy emanating from this sacred place. We placed our hands on the stones and felt the healing energy moving through us and out into the world. We stayed in this place for quite awhile, opening ourselves to let the energy pass through us, learning what it felt like to become more of a hollow bone. Now, she told me, is the time for you to begin the study of energy flow and the ways in which we can use energy for healing and transformation.

The relief contained in that simple thought opened me up. It was the dawning of a new day. If it was time to study energy work, then I could do that. I felt great joy and, in true otter fashion, danced out to the ocean with my otter friend.

Meditation of the West

Prior to beginning the meditation exercise, use the techniques described in Meditation: Basic Tools in the chapter entitled Preparing for Study, part of the Resources section at the end of the book.

Visualize yourself in harmony with all creation, listen to the drum heartbeat of Mother Earth, and use your breath to sink deeper into relaxation and trance.

Breathe light into your body, beginning at your crown and traveling down toward your feet. Consciously relax a particular part of your body with each breath. Draw the energy of Mother Earth, colored a velvety moss green, up through your feet to your pelvis, up into your solar plexus, heart, throat, third eye, and out through the crown of your head. Feel yourself letting go of all judgment. Become a willing observer.

You find yourself standing in the wind on a sandy beach. It is late afternoon and the sinking sun greets you from far out on the ocean's horizon. You are alone here. Behind you a cliff rises high to a forested promontory. The song of the waves lapping the shore and the cries of circling gulls are all that you hear.

Just to the north lie three tree-covered islands, separated by narrow channels. You notice it is almost high tide and time to go. You return to the spot down the beach where you left your kayak beside a running stream and launch, paddling out across the channel and toward the islands.

You dip your paddle in rhythmic strokes, moving further toward your destination. Ahead you see the fins of dolphins moving in unison toward a thin portion of the channel opposite an island's small river outlet. One jumps out of the sea to land again with a resounding splash—sheer exuberance that makes you smile. The dolphins are hunting salmon, and as they circle, working as a team, you can see the silver-sided salmon dodge and turn as one, running hard for the river's mouth.

You reach the mouth of the river and notice hundreds of salmon returning to the place of their birth after years of circling the ocean. There are so many you could almost walk across the river without getting your feet wet. They have come to give away their lives to ensure the next generation. You pull your kayak up on the bank and follow them upriver in the dusk. Like the salmon, you, too, are going home to perform a giveaway.

You walk slowly, deliberately, taking care to make some sound, as you are sure to encounter bear here. As you round a bend in the path, she is there, fishing, almost as if she expected you. She *harummppphs* and deftly catches a fish with one paw, then holds it to the ground until it stops wriggling enough for her to take a bite. You wait, noticing that, strangely enough, she is the only bear fishing tonight at this prime salmon hole.

You stand on the riverbank as the shadows grow deeper, listening to the murmuring river and the wind in the alder. When She-Bear finishes her snack, she walks up to the path

ahead and lumbers onward, upward, following the river. You walk behind her, knowing that when the time is right she will speak to you. After a time you reach a place in the river where there is a small waterfall and rapids. She stands at the riverbank, watching, waiting. You, too, stand still, mesmerized by the continuous stream of water that appears to be coming from a calm pool above, and the rushing sound that seems to calm you.

Dusk descends in full, and She-Bear moves toward the placid pool above the waterfall. You climb down the riverbank and over the river rock to stand where you can see your reflection in the pool. She dips her paw into your reflection, and you note the swirls and eddies that blur your image on the water's mirror surface. You focus your eyes again and your image begins to slowly coalesce and take form. But this image doesn't look quite like the self you remember. And then in the blink of an eye, the reflection becomes crystal clear. It may not be an image you recognize, but there is no mistaking the fact that she is smiling back at you with recognition and deep love. You hear She-Bear say to you, "This is the female that lives within you."

Once again she dips her paw into the reflection, and the image blurs. You focus your eyes again and see another faint shape gradually coalesce and take form. The reflection clears. This may not be an image you recognize either, but there is no mistaking the fact that he means you well, he will help you with anything you ask and will protect you at all costs. You hear She-Bear say to you, "This is the male that lives within you."

She-Bear dips her paw into his reflection. This time the image seems very faint and shadowy. You wonder if it will come back at all. She-Bear asks, "Are you ready to forgive; forgive and let go; forgive and let be; release and re-member and take back yourself?" You nod your head, as the reflection begins to clear. You'll see the image of a woman whom you have known in your past. You may not want to see it, but look

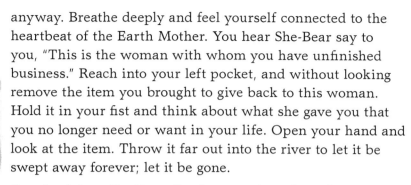

anyway. Breathe deeply and feel yourself connected to the heartbeat of the Earth Mother. You hear She-Bear say to you, "This is the woman with whom you have unfinished business." Reach into your left pocket, and without looking remove the item you brought to give back to this woman. Hold it in your fist and think about what she gave you that you no longer need or want in your life. Open your hand and look at the item. Throw it far out into the river to let it be swept away forever; let it be gone.

One final time She-Bear dips her paw into the reflection. The image emerges slowly, faintly, and finally clears. You'll see the image of a man whom you have known at some time in your life. You hear She-Bear say, "This is the man with whom you have unfinished business." You nod your head in acknowledgment. Breathe deeply. Remember, you are only an observer. Reach into your right pocket, and without looking remove the item you brought to give back to this man. Hold it in your fist and think about what he gave you that you no longer need or want in your life. Open your hand and look at the item. Release it into the river to let it be swept away forever, and let it be gone.

When you turn to look at She-Bear, you realize she is gone. You have completed your task. Reach into your pocket and take out a pinch of tobacco from the packet you keep there. Hold it up to the universe and the first faint stars of dusk, and thank Sister Bear for the gift you have received. Let the tobacco fall from your hand into the river and be swept over the waterfall.

Close your eyes and begin to sink back to this time and place. *(Drumming changes to a different, faster beat for about two minutes to call you back.)* Enter your body in the here and now.

When you are ready, open your eyes. Write down all that you saw and thought, and begin to work on answering the questions on the next page. If there were portions of the meditation that did not seem clear, feel free to do the meditation again another day.

Journal

1. Chronicle your water journey in your journal.

2. Describe in detail the female and male within that She-Bear showed you in the meditation. What are their strengths, heritages, intentions, weaknesses? How are they similar? How are they different? Do you recognize them as parts of yourself?

3. Note your feelings about the woman with whom you have unfinished business. Think about your history with her and the issues between you. Think about what you've learned from her and how, if you had not had her in your life, you would not have experienced something that made you who you are today. Describe the item you threw back into the river and what it meant to let it go.

4. Note your feelings about the man with whom you have unfinished business. Think about your history with him and the issues between you. Think about what you've learned from him and how, if you had not had him in your life, you would not have experienced something that made you who you are today. Describe the item you threw back into the river and what it meant to let it go.

5. Assess your relationship with your dreams. Are they important to you? Do you usually remember them? Do you attribute meaning to them, or associate any patterns between your waking processes and dream processes? Do you keep a dream journal? For this month particularly, use your journal to record dreams and other visions you experience. Identify how these supplement or clarify your work in the West.

6. Think about the mirroring concept, and how you create your own reality. Can you recognize how the people in your life reflect back to you what is within you—how even people you dislike mirror the things you dislike

about yourself? Identify what each important person in your life mirrors back to you, both positive and negative traits. What would you like to change in yourself? How can you begin to accomplish these changes?

7. Describe how you usually deal with your emotions. Do you process on a rollercoaster, or in a bathtub by candlelight? Do you stew about things and keep a bag full of "stuff" to dump out in a diatribe, or do you deal with events as they arise, as honestly as possible? Do you indulge your emotions and catch a high on the drama and the trauma, or do you perhaps deny your feelings in an effort to keep a stiff upper lip?

8. How do you deal with other people's emotions? Are you able to look at cause and effect in relationships with others and accept responsibility, without judgment, for the ways that your actions affect other people in your life? When others' actions affect you, do you blame them and feel victimized, or are you able to look at your own part in the dynamic?

9. On a scale of one to ten, ten being perfection, what is your skill level in reflecting truth in situations that you find hurtful without blaming others? What is your skill level in receiving truth from another without defensiveness? If you feel you need to improve your skills, how will you find the ways to begin this process?

Forgiveness

A Three-Week Written Practice

This exercise involves beginning to forgive three important people in your life. One is the male figure from your past who made himself known to you in your meditation, the second is the female figure from your earlier life who made herself known in your meditation. The third is yourself.

Substitute your own name and the name of the male and female figures in the spots indicated. Invite White Wolf to be your witness.

Week One
Write the same simple phrase seventy times daily
for seven days. The phrase is:
I, **your name***, now forgive* **male figure***. I bless and release you.*

Week Two
Write the same simple phrase seventy times daily
for seven days. The phrase is:
I, **your name***, now forgive* **female figure***. I bless and release you.*

Week Three
Write the same simple phrase seventy times daily
for seven days. The phrase is:
I, **your name***, now forgive* **myself.**
I bless and release myself from the past.

You'll find that your writing may bring up anger or resentment. Work on understanding your process so that you can release what you no longer need.

Identify the events or issues for which you are forgiving yourself and others. Focus on releasing these events and emotions so that something new can move into your life. Remember that acceptance without forgiveness is resignation; resignation can stay with you for a long time, and it can kill your spirit. Sometimes forgiveness is a long-term process; do as much as you can for now and come back to it later.

When you complete this exercise, move on to the ceremony.

Cleansing Ceremony

For a list of tools and general setup instructions, see Basic Tools for Ceremony in the chapter entitled Preparing for Study, part of the Resources section at the end of the book. In addition, for this ceremony you will need access to water—bathtub, ocean, lake, stream, basin or bowl of water—a small mirror, a quartz crystal, and representations of the items you threw into the water during the guided meditation.

Begin this ceremony at dusk, when the sun has gone down but before the stars come out. Build a Medicine Wheel, placing the items you brought in the North, East, and South. In the West, at the perimeter of your Circle, place water of some type—even if it is not within your vision. The source of water can be the ocean, a stream, or some other source; it could even be in another room in your house (like the bathroom with a tub full of water), but it needs to be easily accessible to use as part of the ceremony. Place the crystal in the center of the Circle, with the point up to the sky and the bottom rooted in the Earth (a bowl of earth or sand will suffice if indoors).

Enter the Wheel in the Southwest, just adjacent to the West but not yet using the West gate. Call in the directions beginning with the West, circling the Wheel as you do so. Call in the West in a special way, with a song or prayer that invites the essence of Water, Bear, and Salmon into your Circle. Give thanks for this homecoming, this re-membering of yourself. Walk around the Circle to sit in the East, facing West.

Look at the crystal in the center and sit for a moment or two in silence. Remember your male and female selves that She-Bear showed you at the beginning of your work in the West. Visualize them clearly in your mind and ask them to come and sit beside you in the Circle. Feel their strength and beauty. Know they are a part of you and will help you to release what you no longer need. Know you can call on them for assistance at any time.

Now think for a moment about the male and female figures you worked with in your forgiveness writing exercise. As you see them with your mind's eye, bless them and send them love in the form of light. Say aloud: *"I release you and wish you well. I forgive you and hope you find what you need in this life to make you happy. I thank you for what you've taught me. Our unfinished business is resolved. Any further ties between us will be guided by love."* Repeat this seven times for each individual. Say it, and mean it.

Then walk to the water in the West and wash yourself clean from any unhealthy influence these people may have in your present life. You can immerse fully in the water (preferable) or simply wash your hands—whatever feels most comfortable or necessary. Repeat as often as you like: *"I forgive you and release you,* Name of Person. *I wish you peace and love."* Let the washing transform you and cleanse you. If there are tears, let them come. As you wash, visualize any last encumbrances falling away, and see yourself free from any further negative entanglements with these individuals or events from the past.

When you finish, step out of the water and dry yourself. Walk around the Circle, passing through the North to return to sit in the East, facing West again.

Pick up the mirror you brought and look at yourself. Remember, you are changing, re-membering yourself. You are transmuting your perspective through the power of your forgiveness. You are becoming your vision by healing yourself and your relationships. You are changing the mirror: as you change, the people and situations in your life will change or fade from view.

Close the Circle by releasing each direction you called, in reverse order. Thank the spirits and guides for their support, including the spirits of the land where you spent this time on the

Path of the White Wolf. Leave the site more beautiful than when you found it by placing a small offering, a bundle of herbs, a flower, or a pinch of tobacco.

Record Keepers

Stone People, Record Keepers
Speak to me now
As once you did
In days long ago
When I was but a child
Sitting on the sand
Within your Sacred Circle,
Not yet understanding
Stones can't talk.

I heard you then,
And knew your Power
And the absolute safety
Of your protection,
That within the Circle
I could come to no harm.
You whispered to me
With ancient voices,
The Ancestors calling to me.

In wonder I learned
To remember the songs
Of other lives and times
Long past, in Tribal Memory.
The pictures on your faces
Recalled to me Drums and
Dances around Age-old fires,
And small darkskin people
With spirit-wise visage.

They told me the secrets
Of Alchemy and Sound,
Of shape-shifting
And tricks of light.
They taught of Power
Of dancing the Spirit Dances
Of journeys to the World Below
And the Stars Above Us
Where the Elders dwell.

Within the Body of a stone
I saw the sacred healing moss
Captured for eternity
And was told the secret
For setting its magic free
To cure the Earth's worst ills.
But I've forgotten now
For now I'm an adult,
And I know stones can't heal.

So I come to the Circle
Of Stone People today
And ask you to free me
Of my grown-up masks
And make me a child once more
That I may hear
The healing ways
And bring wholeness
To Mother Earth again.

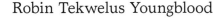

Brothers and Sisters
Join in the Medicine Wheel
With ears to hear
And eyes to see
And voices to send
The fragrance of our prayers
On the wind today
To renew our Mother's life,
That she may live in peace.

Robin Tekwelus Youngblood

Aspects of the North

Element: *Mineral/Stones*
Embodiment: *Mental*
Emotions: *Gratitude/Serenity*
Season: *Winter*
Time: *Night*
Moon Cycle: *New*
Phase of Life: *Elder*
Color: *White*
Creatures: *Standing Ones (trees)*
Expression: *Rattle, Sticks, Bones*
Way: *Mentor*
Place on the Wheel: *Standing in Truth*
Lesson: *Wisdom/Power*
Ceremony: *Prayer Bundles*

Standing in the *North*

In the North you abide in the realm of night, winter, and the new or crescent moon. The North is quiet, and here the mind processes all the information it has been busily gathering. In the North you reap wisdom from experience. In this time you will begin to experience the deep security and personal power that comes from knowing who you are and acknowledging your truth.

With White Wolf at your side, you are well prepared for this part of the journey. In your Medicine Bundle you carry the seed of awareness from the East, the passionate fire of creativity from the South, and the newborn wholeness from introspective healing and release of the past in the West. You understand yourself in a deeper way than ever before. You are ready to receive the wisdom of the North.

Here you connect with the sure and steady essence of the Stone People—those who have witnessed all manner of events, who store information and transform light. Stones are record-keepers and healers. Different stones possess different qualities and attributes that help us accelerate our processes to achieve a particular objective.

The song of the North is the shaking-up sound of rattles or sticks/bones/stones clacked together. This sound has the ability to change the order of things, including thoughts, energy patterns, and emotions. This sound compels you to refocus mentally, thus allowing new wisdom and new perspectives to come to you. The contents (insides) of the rattle itself—sometimes consisting of specific stones—can guide the refocusing process and work with you for purposes of manifestation. While the drum connects you and grounds you, the rattles shake you up and change you in some way; this is a useful balance.

The North is the place of the Standing Ones: trees more ancient than any other living beings. There is great wisdom in their quiet observation; like the Stones, the Trees know all that has gone before.

At this point in your journey, you begin to see that there is a time and a need for those who have experience to speak up and stand tall, to teach and guide the young. The North is the place of mentoring. As a mentor, with your truth and authenticity as well as your understanding of accountability and responsibility, you may give the wisdom gleaned from your experiences to those in need.

In most tribal cultures, the individuals with the most experience and knowledge—usually those of greater years—were community (not war) leaders. The responsibility of leadership was often shared between men and women, and respect was accorded to those who had lived through many seasons. Now, especially in technological cultures, elders live out of the mainstream of life, cut off from family and community. Regrettably, they are unproductive and uninvolved. The North can bring balance to your relationship with elders.

In this quadrant of the Medicine Wheel, you will connect to your elders and ancestors, to those who have come before you and have passed on to you your heritage and lineage for this lifetime. Your ancestors can be powerful guides, mentors, and friends in spirit form. They can share their wisdom and teach you through dreams, visions, and inspiration. Ancestors may be called upon for protection and knowledge. We all come to this lifetime with ancestral knowledge stored in our DNA. The problem is that we have forgotten how to access this wisdom;

we discredit the inner voices we hear, the elder wisdom that speaks to us.

In the North you will discover the wealth of wisdom and experience you have within that you can draw upon for yourself and your children.

North is where you find Buffalo, who teaches GiveAway, community, and prayer. Buffalo provided all manner of subsistence for the people: food, shelter, clothing, tools, and heat. Buffalo teaches that by giving away, you receive. GiveAway means giving freely with an open hand, trusting that the universe will provide abundance. Within the lesson of GiveAway is the wisdom to know when to GiveAway to yourself, that is, when to go to the well and fill up so that you can GiveAway again to others. With Buffalo in the North, we learn to pray in joy and gratitude for all we have received and smoke prayers for All Our Relations in a sacred way.

Path of the White Wolf

Owl also lives in the North. This night bird symbolizes wisdom in many cultures. Owl sees through the darkness and discerns truth in the barest of light. Owl Medicine illuminates unseen truths and brings clarity and focus. We find in the North the ability to discern the truth in any situation and see the light through the darkness of any life circumstance.

Welcome to this journey, to this place on the Wheel on the Path of the White Wolf. Welcome to the teaching of the ancestors and Buffalo, and the essence of Stone People. Welcome to wisdom and authenticity as the Wheel turns in this spiral of learning.

Aho!

White Buffalo Calf Pipe Woman and the Sacred Pipe

White Buffalo Calf Pipe Woman brought the gift of the sacred Pipe to the Lakota (Sioux) peoples. Throughout time, her story has reminded the people to honor the sacredness of life and to walk the Earth in balance with All Our Relations. You can begin to understand her power and beauty as well as the importance of prayer in your life through her story, which we offer here.

As two hunters searched for buffalo out on the plains, they noticed a strange figure moving in the far distance. It was coming directly toward them, surrounded by a bright light. When it came closer they recognized it as a beautiful woman with a bundle on her back.

The two hunters looked upon this woman in very different ways. One approached her with lustful intent and she embraced him in her robe as if in welcome. The other hunter stood aside and watched as mist surrounded her for a moment. When the mist cleared, the women opened her arms to reveal the bones of his hunting partner.

This second man looked at this woman with amazement. He had no intention of harming her, but as with all true warriors, he wished to serve All His Relations in a good way. Recognizing her power, he asked her to come teach his people, and she agreed. He returned to his camp to prepare a Lodge for her and gathered the people to meet her.

She came to the people and opened her bundle to show them the sacred Pipe made of catlinite and the long stem made of wood. She told them to use the Pipe in sacred rites, to remind the people of their oneness and to represent a union of all within the Circle of life. She showed them how to pray with the Pipe, raising their voices to the

Great Spirit. She reminded them that each day is holy, and whatever you do to your relations—animal, winged ones, swimmers, plant, mineral, creepy-crawlers, star beings, ancestors, and generations to come—you do to yourself; we are all connected.

White Buffalo Calf Pipe Woman's message still applies. With this in mind here in the North, you are called to prayer. In these turbulent times we cannot stress enough that prayer is needed. Don't worry about how your prayers sound. Use whatever form of prayer feels right for you. Remember, it is just you and the Great Mystery. Speak from your heart. Keep it simple, keep it clear. Pray with gratitude for what you have and for what you envision. Pray for self, loved ones, community, world, All Our Relations, and the Earth. Pray for highest truth, greatest good, only love, harm to none. Pray in your car or in the shower or eating dinner, anywhere, anyplace, anytime.

The Story of Robin's Pipe

The ancestors brought the sacred Pipe to Robin a few years after she reached adulthood. The story of this event illustrates how our elders continue to speak to us from the Other Side Camp (spirit world). As you move around the Wheel, you will recognize synchronicity and magic in your life with more and more frequency; you will find that you can tap in to the wisdom of your guides and ancestors. The exercises in this chapter help you connect more deeply to your own DNA wisdom.

I went to an Indian art auction, a sale of Native American artifacts, usually collected by Caucasians and sold for profit. I was uncomfortable to be in such an environment, but wanted to see what they had and perhaps buy a Pendleton blanket. Instead, a beautiful buckskin-fringed bag beaded with a very old design attracted my eye. It called to me, insistently, from across the room. I opened the bidding on the piece and got it for the opening price because no one else bid.

When I went to collect this treasure, the auctioneer felt some-thing in the bag. Opening it, he withdrew a small and beautifully made Pipe. "Lady," he said, "if I had known this was in the bag, there's no way you would have gotten it for this price!" I smiled, reached for the bag, thanked him, and left.

For years I held the Pipe in awe and reverence, never using it. I didn't know what to do with it. Eventually, I began to question my elders. One told me to "ask the Pipe why it has come to you." After doing this, I began to see an elder woman in my dreams, and she gave me instructions in the way this Pipe is to be used, and told me to use it for my family. (In Indian ways, family is a very extended term.)

As I began to do ceremony with this Pipe for myself and the women of my tiyospaye (extended family), others began to see this old woman standing with the Pipe. Finally, an Indian elder in my circle asked me if I had seen her. When I answered that I had, she asked if I knew who she was. I told her I thought I did, but would like to know for sure. Auntie said to me, "This woman is your great-grandmother, and this Pipe belonged to your family. It has been returned to you. Use it well."

I have carried this Pipe with deep humility for over twenty years now, and my great-grandmother still sits with it. Her teachings have upheld me on my path all along the way. Throughout the years I have seen many prayers answered through this Pipe: cancer healed, runaway children brought home, addictions released. I give thanks to the ancestors and spirit beings who brought it home and charged me with the responsibility of carrying it.

Meditation of the North

Prior to beginning the meditation exercise, use the techniques described in Meditation: Basic Tools in the chapter entitled Preparing for Study, part of the Resources section at the end of the book.

Visualize yourself in harmony with all creation, listen to the drum heartbeat of Mother Earth, and use your breath to sink deeper into relaxation and trance. *(Drum a minute or so.)*

Breathe brilliant white light into your body, beginning at your head and traveling down toward your feet. Consciously relax a particular part of your body with each breath. Draw the energy of Mother Earth, colored a velvety moss green, up through your feet to your pelvis, up into your solar plexus, heart, throat, third eye, and out through the crown of your head. Feel yourself letting go of all judgment. Become a willing observer. Surround yourself with a rose-quartz egg, which emanates love and protects you from any unwanted energy.

You find yourself standing knee-deep in frost-laden golden grass on a vast rolling plain that stretches in all directions as far as your eyes can see. It is winter, dry and clear with a slight breeze. The temperature is cold but you are dressed warmly, and you set out up a slight hill to gain a higher vantage. As you reach the top you realize that although it may seem flat, the plain is not one big field but actually rolling hills broken here and there by rocky outcroppings and cut-away streambeds. You take a blanket from your pack and sit cross-legged on the hilltop, facing north to survey the landscape. The sun warms your back, and you think of how many others may have sat in this same place to seek wisdom and guidance.

You hear a sound like thunder and look to the sky, but it remains clear. You note that the sound persists and seems to

be getting louder, and then you see them in the distance: running buffalo. Their strength and beauty is astounding. You notice how the herd runs as a unit behind a mature female, turning in unison. They cross a streambed and come toward your hilltop, passing through the small valley below and moving south. The Earth itself seems to reverberate with the sound of their hooves—a sound that seems to pass through you and around you and permeate your very being. You feel a strange, jolting wrench and turn to look behind you. You wonder how you could have sat here so long and never noticed you were not alone.

Behind you stretch a long line of beings, most of them elders, grandmothers or grandfathers. It is your own ancestral lineage. You stand and step forward to meet the woman or man at the front of the line. You recognize her or him as your own mother or father, and take her or his hand for a moment, thanking her or him for the opportunity she or he gave you to come into this lifetime.

You then step forward to meet your grandmother or grandfather. This may be someone you know already or someone whom you never met before. You look into your grandparent's eyes and take his or her hand for a moment. In that moment you see in your mind's eye a picture of who this being is or was, and you'll know whether this is the elder from whom you have come to learn on this day.

Repeat this with your great-grandparent, great-greatgrandparent, and all the rest, until you come to an individual with whom you feel a strong connection—someone who might understand you if they were a part of your life now. When you reach this one, you'll instinctively recognize the elder you are seeking on this journey. As you hold the elder's hand and catch a view of who he or she is and was, and what the elder stood for in his or her life, record this in your memory for later. Spend a little time drinking in the essence of your lineage as this elder shares it with you. Enjoy it, feel

its power, strength, courage, and love, the embodiment of all generations. Then silently ask your elder what qualities from your lineage you embody, what strengths you have inherited that you may not already know about. After you receive this information, look deeply into the elder's eyes and thank him or her.

Now look ahead at the line of ancestors before you. This is your lineage, your inheritance. Absorb through your very pores the essence of your foremothers and forefathers. Have you ever been any of your progenitors? If you have, step into that body for a moment, wherever it stands along your line, and feel your presence there. Feel the lessons of that lifetime, your courage and endurance. You are not here to relive ancient pain, only to review the circumstances that built your character. Let the pictures of the past flow through without attachment.

Listen to the heartbeat of the mother and breathe deeply. Have you been both your own grandfather and grandmother? A male body feels and acts differently than a female. Step into the roles of each for a moment. After you take a moment with this, return to the hilltop.

Close your eyes and hear the sound of buffalo hooves pounding the earth and surging through you. Follow the sound and go back as far as your mind will take you, back to the beginning, the first place your spirit has ever known. See yourself moving from Source into body. Who were your first parents? Were they star beings or humans—or both? Allow yourself to see them in great detail. What was the color of their hair? Eyes? What were they wearing, if anything? What shapes were their bodies?

As you record these memories, begin to broaden your view to take in the surroundings. Ask Sister Owl to help you with this. What kind of landscape did your first ancestors' spirits emanate from? Was it harsh or tropical? Green or arid? File these snapshots in your mind for further evaluation.

Remember that this is spiral time—past, present, and future are one. You are able at this time to experience both your forebears and your descendants. At some point in the future, you may be one of your great-grandchildren, nieces, nephews, or cousins. In this instant you can implant your present and accumulated knowledge in the DNA of one of your future family members. It is their inheritance. Communicate with this being all that you would like to see happen in his or her generation to balance and heal the Earth. Feel your connection to all beings throughout time and space. Know the completeness of your life through all lives.

Hear the beat of the drum, reconnect to your body, and sink back to this time and place. *(Drumming changes to a different, faster beat for a minute or so to call the journeyer back.)* Enter your body in the here and now.

When you are ready, open your eyes. Write down all that you saw and thought, and begin to work on answering the questions in the next section.

Journal

1. After the meditation, use your journal to chronicle this journey with your ancestors. What information did you receive from the elder with whom you connected?

2. What is your own ancestral lineage? What do you know about your family—its history, stories, trials, and successes? What did you learn about your lineage from the meditation to supplement information you already know? What strengths do you embody from your lineage? Has anyone in your family researched your family's genealogy? What can you learn from them?

3. Revisit some of the work you did in the East. Review your list of strengths and abilities. Review the 21-day essay work you accomplished in the East.

4. Use your journal to record dreams and other visions experienced during this time. Identify how these enrich or clarify your work in the North.

5. Research various crystals and gemstones and their properties. Which do you find yourself attracted to and why?

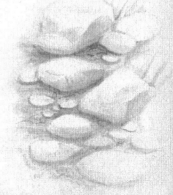

6. How have you learned to pray? What does this mean to you?

The Being You
Were Born to Be

A Three-Week Written Practice

For the teachings in the North, there are two written exercises.

The first exercise will help you to reclaim yourself, to rediscover the being you were born to be and your true strengths and abilities. Your work in the East began this process. Here in the North your acceptance of the vision of who you are and who you will be deepens. Take the help of White Wolf, who totally accepts his majestic beauty. Allow this exercise to reveal the beauty, power, and wisdom of your highest, unchanging self.

Week One

You will write the same simple phrase 28 times
daily for seven days.
I, **your name**, *recognize the power, beauty, and wisdom
of the being I was born to be.*

Week Two

You will write the same simple phrase 28 times
daily for seven days.
I, **your name**, *begin to claim the power, beauty, and wisdom
of the being I was born to be.*

Week Three

You will write the same simple phrase 28 times
daily for seven days.
I, **your name**, *now claim the power, beauty, and wisdom
of the being I was born to be.*

You may find yourself feeling some resistance as you write. Resistance can also manifest in three-dimensional reality through events that seem to prove you are *not* what you are claiming. It is your ego or subconscious that rejects change as it tries to hold on to the old, familiar you. Focus, and stick with your work. You *are* changing from the inside out. Don't be discouraged. Observe your process, including resistance, so you can release what you determine you no longer need.

To complete the second exercise, over the next three weeks make two lists. One list will reflect a goal you plan to accomplish in the next year (or a few goals, depending on your preference). This goal should be definite and concrete, a specific and creative endeavor that moves you out of your comfort zone. Your goal will redefine you and represent the power, beauty, and wisdom of your unique individuality. Really think about this as you do the exercise "The Being You Were Born to Be." This goal can be a significant step toward a larger life goal.

The second list will name all the reasons why you think you can't accomplish the goal(s). You will need to release each of these reasons before you can get there from here. This list may include patterns that no longer serve you, behaviors that sabotage you, and/or beliefs that limit you. Save these lists for use in the integration ceremony.

Prayer Bundle Ceremony

For a list of tools and general setup instructions, see Basic Tools for Ceremony in the chapter entitled Preparing for Study, part of the Resources section at the end of the book. For the Prayer Bundle Ceremony you will create two bundles.

1. You'll need two 12 by 12 inch pieces of white cotton cloth, two different colors of string, and the two lists you made in the second exercise.

2. Collect the following items to be placed in the bundles (items must be burnable and biodegradable).

   • For bundle number one, collect one or more items that symbolize the Being You Were Born to Be, and the list of goals you prepared. Bring a stick to use as a prayer arrow. Decorate the prayer arrow any way you want, giving it your energy and attention and making it beautiful and sacred.

   • For bundle number two, collect one or more items that symbolize what prevents you from becoming the Being You Were Born to Be, and the list of stuff you need to release to accomplish your goals.

Be sure to bring some dried cedar for smudge. You will also need four special Stone People to represent the four cardinal directions. You may find them in your garden, at the beach, or on a hike.

After preparing for the ceremony as outlined in Basic Tools for Ceremony, build a small fire, big enough to burn one of your prayer bundles but not so large that you will have trouble putting it out or that it will burn for a long time. Be sure to employ all appropriate safety precautions. The fire will be the center of the Circle for the ceremony. If you are performing the ceremony indoors, use a candle for the center and a fireplace or other safe alternative for burning one of the bundles.

Sit in the South and, using your rattle to open the Circle, call in the essence of each direction: East, South, West, North, Above, Below, and Center. Place one special stone in each cardinal direction, and call in the properties or spirit of the stone to assist you and bear witness. When you invite the spirit of the stone into the Circle, speak the attributes the stone represents for you. For example, a large white stone placed in the North might represent the strength and majesty of a mountain. Be sure to call in Buffalo and Owl, representing the lessons of GiveAway and discernment, and your ancestors.

Take out the items for the prayer bundles. Beginning with the bundle containing the list of what you need to release, use cedar to smudge the bundle wrapping and the items to be placed inside. Really think about what each piece means. Bless the challenges represented by each item assembled for this first bundle. Pray in thankfulness for the lessons you've learned on your path. Smudge the list as you read it one last time. Pray for assistance from your ancestors, grandmothers, and grandfathers. Then place all items in the bundle, affix it to the arrow/stick, and tie it closed.

Repeat the same sequence for the second bundle with your list of goals, blessing your vision for yourself, the goal for the next year, and the teachings yet to come. Did you remember the two colored strings? Use them here to remind you which bundle is which.

Now take the bundles and sit at the other side of the fire, in the North. Offer a prayer to your ancestors and tell them what you are doing. Ask for their blessings. Take the first prayer bundle containing the list of obstacles and release it into the fire. As the fire burns the bundle, visualize everything that you wish to release going up in smoke. Sit quietly in prayer for a few moments. Offer gratitude for your life and your blessings. Pray humbly for wisdom, understanding, healing, or whatever you need right now. Release what no longer serves you. Take as long as you need. Connect with the spirit of Buffalo to witness your GiveAway.

Now hold the second bundle with the list of goals you want to accomplish. Visualize the tasks you have set as accomplished by the Being You Were Born to Be. Envision your goals and dreams for the next year. Pray for the strength and teachings to accomplish all you need to, and to make your vision manifest. This is the first act of the Being You Were Born to Be, the first manifestation of the new you. Pray to the ancestors for help and to your guides to watch over you as you move out into the world in a new way. Pray out loud or silently to yourself. Take as long as you need. Connect with the spirit of Owl to help you discern truths as you walk your new path. Tie the bundle to the prayer arrow.

When you are finished praying, sit in silence a few moments and ask the ancestors if they have any messages for you. Open your mind and heart to receive. After a few minutes, open your eyes and observe your environment. Does anything catch your attention? If so, make a note of it.

Close the Circle by releasing, in reverse order, each direction and each helper you called to the Circle. Thank them for their support. Thank White Wolf for the path you are walking. Put out the fire (do this safely) and pack up your belongings.

After the ceremony, leave the second prayer arrow bundle somewhere that calls to you, preferably a place that is out of the way of traffic and is sacred to you. Be sure that the prayer arrow is pointed up to send your prayer to the universe. Release it to the Great Mystery—let it fly—then celebrate!

Journey

Drumming, Chanting,
Humming song,
I journey to the void,
The Soul's world
Far from this world.

Trancing, Drifting,
Meditating now,
I see the Panther
Power and Grace
Leading me.

Gliding, Sliding,
Swimming through Air,
I follow the Owl
Through day-lit night
Wandering aloft.

Magical, Mystical,
Crystal home
Tipi of tranquility
Glowing in clarity
Beckoning me.

Conical, Spherical,
Geometrical shapes.
Colors making sounds,
Sounds into waves
Crashing ashore.

Electrical, Symmetrical,
Retractile light,
Powering the cosmos
Shattering my eyes
Reforming knows.

Playing, Imagining,
Meandering through
The menagerie of netherland,
Spirit animals each
Bringing new.

Renewing, Reliving,
Experiencing all,
Learning to balance
While upside down,   *Falling, Leaping,*
Beginning now.   *Diving upright,*
    Being pulled once again
    To the morning's light,
    Journey's end.

Robin Tekwelus Youngblood

Aspects of Above

Element: *Space*
Embodiment: *Ethereal Body*
Emotions: *Lightness/Emptiness*
Season: *Eternal*
Time: *Timeless*
Moon Cycle: *Void of Course*
Phase of Life: *Perpetual*
Color: *Indigo*
Creatures: *Star People*
Expression: *Sounding/Toning*
Way: *Union with the Void*
Place on the Wheel: *Openness*
Lesson: *Universal Consciousness*
Ceremony: *Star Wheel*

Traversing Above

Above the Wheel is the realm of time-without-time. Sky Father, the keeper of Great Mystery, leads you into the void, the state of ageless wisdom, the place before beginning. All the answers to all questions ever asked are found here. In this domain you connect with the ancestors who, many believe, came from the Star Nations to populate our planet. Here dwells the eternal all-and-nothing, the Universal Mind, or Universal Consciousness.

Attunement with Universal Mind begins in repose, before creative action. Open your eyes with the awareness of the East, inhale the creativity of the South. Practice the stillness that you learned in the West, and dwell in silence. Call in the ancestors you met in the North. Was one a star being?

In the Above, you can perceive the crack between the worlds, where past, present, and future merge into the now. The color indigo of deepest space pervades this dimension, where there are galaxies, black holes, and infinite mystery. To be in this place is to experience pure emptiness, an extraordinary lightness of being.

"As without, so within." Your quest is to merge with the Great Mysterious Void, which is both inside and outside. Through emptiness, you will discover your fullness.

In union with Universal Consciousness, you release all concepts, beliefs, and cultural perspectives. You must be willing to go beyond anything you have ever known to experience this conjunction. If you hold too tightly to preconceptions about the meaning and purpose of existence, spirituality, and God, you will try to avoid the teachings and exercises in this chapter. You might wonder whether there is *anything out there* to link with, or if your old, familiar skills can be used in new ways.

The Great Spirit has no name or ideology, and defies definition.

The Great Mystery is everywhere, yet we most often associate it with the Above Direction. All who have reached mastery on the earth plane dwell in the heavenly Lodge with beings of pure spirit. These ancestral teachers, who reside in the abode of the Sky People, communicate with us from the Other Side Camp, the place where we, too, will abide after leaving our bodies.

The moon is void-of-course in the Above, where you will come into relationship with That-Which-Has-No-Form. The akashic records, which chronicle the universe and have been stored in the stars since before the beginning of time, are open and available to you now.

Your connection with this sacred direction allows you to move into a deeper level of awareness and familiarity with your timeless self. In the space of the Above, you can easily extend your awareness outside of your physical body to your etheric and astral bodies, and experience yourself as energy inhabiting physical form. You will know without a doubt that events happen on both visible and invisible levels, and are not always as they appear.

Three-dimensional reality is only one facet of reality. As you become more fully present and the channel to your higher self opens up, you may struggle with discerning exactly how you are receiving information and what to do about it after you get it. Just stay grounded and fully present without judgment, an impartial observer. Remember what you have learned from your journey so far: all paths of expression are teachings.

The song of the Sky Father is a toning sound that comes from deep within the throat: it vibrates and resonates within your very bones. This is universal language, understood long before we two-leggeds created a separate reality. Once we were part of a united whole. In our desire to learn and experience physical manifestation, we created diversity. The music of the spheres is celestial, harmonious, and blends with the resonance of creation. This sound permeates matter and can transform and heal.

Welcome once again to your first home, brothers and sisters. Return to the expansive, unlimited realm of space. Welcome to the teaching of the Stars and the essence of the Void. Welcome to the Alpha and the Omega.

Aho!

Pleiades

A loose cluster of stars in the direction of the constellation Taurus form a group named after the Seven Sisters of Greek mythology. These stars, the Pleiades, are surrounded by a keen nebulosity that shines due to their reflected light. For centuries humankind has gazed in wonder at their beauty. A well-known Cherokee tale presents the origin of the Pleiades.

Seven boys refused to do the chores their mothers asked of them and played games instead. When their mothers determined to feed them stones rather than corn—since they had neglected the cornfields—they decided they would find somewhere else to go, where they would no longer be any trouble to anyone.

They began a dance, whirling round and round, praying to the spirits for help. They danced and danced until their feet no longer touched the ground, and they were suspended in the air. Their mothers came to find them, and still they danced, already almost out of reach.

One mother was able to reach her son with a stick and pull him to earth, but the earth swallowed him whole. The boys rose further and further into the sky, where we see them now as the Pleiades or, as the Cherokee call them, The Boys.

The people grieved for their children, but none more than the mother whose son fell back to earth and disappeared. The following spring, the people noticed a small green plant growing from the spot where he had fallen. The plant grew tall into what we know now as the pine tree, whose essential nature is that of the Pleiades.

Many indigenous people believe that the Pleiades were their ancestral planetary home. Numerous creation stories depict the people coming down to the earth from a "hole in the sky." Both Cherokee and Greek myths depict that the Pleiades originated as earth-dwellers who "returned" to the sky. Some new age practitioners support the Earth-Pleiades connection, reciting personal experiences, including dreams and meditations, which connect with this star system.

Robin's experience, detailed below, takes us on a journey into the realm of space and sky to a place in the Pleiades where ancient wisdom rules peacefully.

Several years ago, before the movie Contact was even imagined, a friend gave me a new age meditation gimmick called The Traveler. It was a device that had an audio track and 3-D glasses. I put the glasses on and started the machine. While it played soft, ethereal music, colored lights blinked onto my closed eyelids at varying rates of speed. As the beat increased, I suddenly found myself traveling through space at an incredible rate —so fast that I could hardly feel the motion—in a vehicle made of some material very similar to human or animal skin (perhaps shark). Suddenly a docking station appeared before my eyes, and we floated soundlessly toward it as if magnetized.

Once landed, I was met by a beautiful individual with very white hair and translucent skin, wearing a shimmering, silvery, luminescent robe with a hood. He or she (I couldn't tell what gender this being was) motioned for me to follow, and then passed through a round portal. When I approached the portal, I saw what appeared to be glass, but upon reaching out to touch it, I found that my hand penetrated the material. I steeled myself and passed to the other side.

There I found myself in a beautiful room, sparsely furnished with some kind of reclining chair, a small table, and a waterfall-

cum-fountain-cum-washbasin. The being washed her/his hands, then signaled me to step into the waterfall and bathe, telepathically communicating that I must be cleansed of any contaminants from my world. I disrobed, entirely without embarrassment. Once I had finished bathing, the being gave me a robe similar to the one he/she was wearing, except that mine was gold in color.

Next we passed through another portal, and my guide smiled as I gasped in astonishment. I had just entered a new world. Many things were similar to our earth environment. I had stepped onto a street in what appeared to be a fairly large city—but what a city! It was sparkling clean, the air was iridescent, and the people walked by or worked on their projects completely at ease and in peace. Everywhere I wandered, I saw beings who emanated joy from the core! When I asked about this, my mentor explained (this was all without the spoken word) that each individual born here understood his purpose from birth, and everything that he did from that point on supported his purpose. Therefore, each being began and lived in harmony. Since each one was following his personal manna, the entire community worked as one, with no separation. This society no longer even had words for war or disharmony; there had been no strife here for centuries.

When I told my guide that we needed the secrets of their culture on earth, he/she smiled somewhat sadly, and with great tolerance said, "You already have these secrets. You just are unwilling to use them. We brought you here today so that you could open your eyes to what you already know deep inside. Go home now, and begin your work."

With her words, I found myself back in the skinpod ship, zooming through space until I was back in my living room.

A few years later as I sat watching Contact on the big screen, I poked the friend I had gone to the theater with and whispered, "I've been there! I've been there!"

The message is clear: We on earth will not find harmony until we each acknowledge and carry out our individual and unique purpose for existence.

Meditation of the Above

Prior to beginning the meditation exercise, use the techniques described in Meditation: Basic Tools in the chapter entitled Preparing for Study, part of the Resources section at the end of the book.

Visualize yourself in harmony with the universe. Listen to the drum heartbeat of Mother Earth *(Drum in a slow two-beat pattern.)* and use your breath to sink deeper into relaxation and trance. Breathe deeply, consciously relaxing a different part of your body with every breath. Surround yourself with a glowing amethyst egg, knowing that you are protected within this egg from any negative energy.

You now find yourself sitting cross-legged at the center of the cosmos. It is the darkest night of the year. Listening, you hear nothing—an absolute absence of sound. Slowly you become aware of the myriad stars twinkling above. You are in a state of No Mind: thoughts drift through but nothing stays. Allow yourself to be without doing.

Gradually you notice a sound floating toward you. There are no words to describe it—music without notes, harmonies without words. A face appears on the blank screen of your mind. You may recognize this being. It may be one of your ancestors or a spirit guide you have worked with before. The essence of this entity shines with peace. This presence has information for you, and all you have to do is receive it. Relax. Go deeper into the silence. Tell your guide that you are willing to hear all that it has to say. *(Drum for a minute or so.)*

It is time to travel. Look within yourself until you locate the silver cord at the base of your spine. Allow your ethereal body to take hold of the cord as you gradually ascend up and out of your body. Keeping hold of the cord, take the hand

of your spirit friend in your other hand. Journey with your guide to a new corner of the universe. Take note of the things you see and experience on your voyage: lights, colors, sounds, encounters with other beings. Store in memory any new information that you receive. You can retrieve it later.

Now, following the silver cord, allow your guide to return you gently to your body. As you arrive, look at your body— really look. *(Faster drumming for a minute or so.)* Admire the color of your hair, your skin tone, the suppleness of your musculature. See the beauty of the being you have chosen to be in this lifetime.

Breathe deeply and feel the reassurance your spirit guide is sending you in tune with the heartbeat of the universe. Hear the drum. Feel yourself as an integral, necessary part of the universe, and look now at the events of your life so far. Don't judge them—just see the pictures as they flow into and out of your mind. See the patterns. See the way that who you are connects with the rest of the web of creation. Understand and accept that everything that has happened in your life has been necessary, for you and for all the others with whom you interact.

Relax and breathe deeply as you reenter your body, still sitting in the center of the universe. Feel the ground beneath you; pat your body to feel how solid it is. Thank your guide for the gifts you have received by touching your fist to your heart, signifying that your heart is full and you are grateful.

Your friend smiles, looks at you one more time with intensity and understanding, then fades into the distance. *(Drumbeat changes to a more rapid beat for a minute or so, to call the journeyer back.)* Remembering all that happened as you traveled, begin to arouse your body in the here and now.

When you are ready, open your eyes. Write down all that you saw and thought, and begin to work on answering the questions on the next page.

Journal

1. In your journal, chronicle your journey with your spirit guide and the connection you made with Universal Mind.

2. List any new information that came through to you from your visit to the star realms. Do you see how it applies to your life? Has any of this information guided you to discard old beliefs and replace them with new perspectives? How?

3. Take an evening to observe the night sky. What attracts your eye? Why? Research the meaning of stars and planets in different cultures. Which tradition best expresses your feeling and understanding about the Above? Why?

4. List the life events you reviewed in this guided meditation. Write down information you received about these events. Each day this month, review these teachings and note in your journal any new memories and details that come up.

5. Record in your journal dreams and other visions experienced during this time. Identify how these clarify and enhance your work with the Above.

6. Contemplate your relationship to space and spaciousness. In your journal, define what *space* is for you.
Observe the sensations and thoughts that arise as you think about the word *void*. Write down what you observe. Describe your relationship to silence.

7. Assess your ability to be alone and still. How does it make you feel?

8. Define what *Mystery* means to you. Do you make room in your life to connect to Mystery? How? When? Do you invite magic, mystery, and inspiration to assist you in finding answers to questions or challenges? How?

Creative Chaos

A Three-Week Written Practice

Our human brains have two sides that, when used together in balance, make us whole, fully alive, and conscious. Yet we predominantly use only one side. This exercise will tap in to both sides of your brain, and in the process will reveal hidden and valuable aspects residing within you. The process entails stream-of-consciousness writing for approximately 10 minutes per day for 21 days—preferably at the same time each day. You will not only be writing about whatever comes to mind, but you will write with your non-dominant hand; that is, if you normally write with your right hand, use your left hand. This is an exercise in cross training.

The 21 topics, one for each day, are:

- Chaos
- Choice
- Life Purpose
- Pleasure and Pain
- Vision
- Attachment and Detachment
- Responsibility
- Creativity
- Destruction
- Guidance
- Surrender
- Spiritual Practices
- Dreaming
- Universal Consciousness

- Ritual
- Mystery
- Connection
- The Void
- Eternal Now
- Silence
- You are all that Is, functioning beautifully in Creative Chaos

Some of what you write may seem silly or not make sense; it may seem like someone other than you is doing the writing. Never mind. Just keep writing. And if a subject is particularly emotional, stop writing and return to it the next day. Don't give up. Become aware of White Wolf as witness. He will help you observe your process and understand your reactions and responses so you can release what you no longer need. As you do this work, prepare a list of issues, memories, or life experiences you wish to release (past situations, old loves, resistant emotions). When you complete this three-week process, move on to the integration ceremony. Save the Creative Chaos essay completed on the twenty-first day for use in the integration ceremony.

Star Wheel Ceremony

For a list of tools and general setup instructions, see Basic Tools for Ceremony in the chapter entitled Preparing for Study, part of the Resources section at the end of the book. In addition, for this ceremony you will need to consider the following.

- Choose a private site where you can see the stars to welcome Sky-Father-Above-Us.
- Bring a portable altar, seven candles, and a small container.
- Have your journal and Creative Chaos essay at hand.

Set up your altar in the late afternoon, just before dusk. Place each candle in a container so the wind won't blow it out. Place one candle in each cardinal direction. Place three candles on a small raised altar in the center of the Wheel to signify Father Sky, Mother Earth, and your highest self.

Call in the Seven Directions, starting with the East. Call in the Star Nation or planet that you associate with each direction. Light the candles as you call in each direction. Then light the candles in the Center Direction. Call in all your ancestors and guides from the Star Nations. Ask them to witness this ceremony and grant their blessings and protection.

Read your Creative Chaos essay aloud to yourself, holding in your consciousness as you read that you *are* all that is.

Lie in the center of the Circle and look up at the stars and moon. Breathe deeply as you relax completely, your eyes open to the stars. If needed, cover yourself with a blanket for warmth.

Close your eyes and think about the silver cord at the base of your spine, which you saw in meditation. Allow your ethereal body to take hold of the cord as you gradually ascend up and out of your body. Holding the cord, look at your surroundings: observe the stars and moon above you and your body below you, lying in the Circle. Still holding the cord, allow yourself to experience this state for a few minutes. Then return to your physical body and sit for awhile in the state of No Mind, allowing the Star Nations and Great Mystery to fill your being with peace. Open your eyes when you are ready.

Take the list of issues, memories, and/or life experiences you made during your essay work. Read over the items you wish to release, as you focus on being in the Now. See the significance or insignificance of each from this perspective. Bless each situation, person, thought, and emotion, asking for peace, health, and happiness to infuse each one. Smudge the list. Know that your spirit is now free of all negativity.

Look around for a *wotai*, a stone memento of this experience. Place it in your Medicine Bag or personal bundle to remind you that you live only Now. Acknowledge yourself in gratitude for the new pathway you are walking. If possible, leave a token of thanksgiving in a nearby tree before you go (in exchange for what you have been given)—something that reminds you of the stars.

Close the Circle by releasing, in reverse order, each direction you called to the Circle, and thank them for their support. Leave the site a little more beautiful than when you found it.

Earthwomb

Deep, deep, deep
In the darkness of night
I sit in timeless stillness inside an Earth Lodge
Lit only by the muted glow of hot stones,
Grandmothers see me.

I am strong, but I feel weak.
I am wise, but I feel ignorant.
I am beautiful, but I feel ugly.
I am finding my way home.

Deep, deep, deep
Steam wafts around my body
Creating rivulets of purifying sweat,
Tears flow freely in understanding release,
Grandmothers hear me.

I am the drummer and I hold the drum,
I am the singer and I sing the songs,
I am the dreamer and I seek the dream,
I am finding my way home.

Deep, deep, deep
Within my heart, mind, and soul
I pray for guidance with grateful

Acknowledgment of all that was, is, and will be,
Grandmothers pray with me.

I am alone, yet I am connected.
I am afraid, yet I am calm.
I am within, yet my spirit soars.
I am finding my way home.

Deep, deep, deep
From the womb of the Earth
I sense her arms open to embrace me.
There is only here and now,
Grandmothers speak to me.

I am the willer and I am the will.
I am the giver and I am the gift.
I am the question and I am the answer.
I am finding my way home.

Sandy D'Entremont

Element: *Organic*
Embodiment: *Source of Life*
Emotions: *Acceptance/Earthiness*
Season: *A Full Year's Cycle*
Time: *Midnight*
Moon Cycle: *Dark*
Phase of Life: *Inception*
Color: *Moss Green*
Creatures: *Subterraneans*
Expression: *Tears*
Way: *Embryo/Birth and Rebirth*
Place on the Wheel: *Initiation*
Lesson: *The Pregnancy of Possibility*
Ceremony: *Earth Lodge*

Grounding

Mother Earth is the womb from which we come. She is the source and fertility. Mother Earth is Below the Medicine Wheel, as the supporting foundation. Within her is the embryonic seed, which contains the genetic encoding of all creation. Once planted, the seed grounds and sends forth its roots deep into the Mother. The genesis has begun.

Your Medicine Bundle is nearly complete. From your journey with White Wolf around the Medicine Wheel you already carry the seed of awareness, the trust of a child, the healthy maturity of adulthood, the voices of the ancestors as they speak their wisdom, and a growing connection to Universal Mind. In the Below direction, you will add only a pinch of soil, which is all that is needed for grounding.

Now it is time to anchor everything you've learned and bring it fully into physical form. It is important not only that you work to stay rooted in the physical world, but that you also use physical activity to help bring yourself totally into your body.

Earth is the source of all nourishment, the embodiment of life-giving Life. She accepts all that we are and all that we are not. She has unending compassion and patience. She is devoid of judgment. To work with the Below, you must understand that each act of creation carries within it initiation.

You must now go to the Earth Lodge, release fear, and submit in trust to this age-old process. In this phase, travelers on the path often rest in the darkness not knowing how the seed within will germinate, but trusting that it will. Pregnant with possibility, you cannot see how the form of your creation will manifest. How and when will your vision be born?

Sometimes in the dark, you experience the salty life-fluid of your tears. These tears are cleansing, warm and soft, gently liberating. They are the sign of surrender to forces greater than yourself.

Your role in the underground world is that of the zygote; you are the embryo fertilized and growing, dependent on forces outside of yourself. At the same time, you are pregnant with creation. In the Below, you are the initiated and the initiator. You are the expectant mother and the fertilized egg. And the assistance of the Most Loving Mother—our Earth Mother—is integral to birthing your heart's desire into physical form. As in any birth process, you need the experience of the wise-woman to ground and guide you.

The lesson of the Below is in your surrender to all possibilities without judgment, particularly self-judgment. Again, White Wolf is your guide. His oneness with the Earth is complete. He never judges himself. Only in becoming more like the Earth Mother and employing compassion, patience, and acceptance toward self will you surrender and allow yourself to experience your highest good with joy.

While in one sense you are the mother and you are being reborn, so also you are the child. Delivery through the womb requires willingness to surrender, trusting that all will be well. Occasionally, surrender means understanding that a particular desire is not in your best interest, and releasing your attachment to it. Sometimes it means accepting responsibility for an unwanted lesson or a task you came into this lifetime to accomplish. If what you want to create will serve you and the Mother best, she will support your desires. In any case you can rest in the Mother, knowing that she will supply all that you need. Acquiescence is the essence of the Below.

Ask yourself whether what you are doing will serve All Your Relations in a meaningful and important way. Are you using the gifts spirit gave you? If you can answer yes, or at least admit true willingness, then you can move forward.

White Wolf's teaching of Below is that every nation, species, and family on earth is necessary: there are no greater or lesser beings than yourself, only beings with more perceptible impact than others. Each nation, each species or family of two-leggeds, winged ones, four-leggeds, swimming ones, standing ones, and plant people, the earth and her subterraneans and all creepy-crawlers, star beings and those who dwell in spirit—each brings unique gifts to our planet.

The Earth Mother nurtures all of us through every season. She dwells within the ripening of all cycles—from inception to seedling, seedling to bud, bud to fully mature flower, fading flower to death—again and again. This is another image of the Wheel of Life.

Mother Earth's essence is organic, supporting growth. Her special people are the subterraneans who aerate the soil, enrich the humus, fertilize the plant people. Ants, worms, mushrooms, moss—these are her favorites! The colors of the Mother are the subtle greens of moss and the rich, dark brown of loam.

Many ancient agrarian peoples prepared for planting with a ceremonial offering at midnight on the dark of the moon. When you approach the Earth Mother, bring an offering to signify your respect and honor her for providing abundance for all her creatures. You are here to ask her help in shaping your heart's desire, in bringing your creation into the world. Look for a natural gift that you can share with her, remembering that she is *your* Mother.

Welcome to this journey, to this place on the Wheel once again. Welcome to the teaching of earth, of Below: surrender and initiation. Welcome to acceptance, compassion, and grounding as the Wheel turns in this cycle of learning.

Aho!

Our Beginnings

When you connect with the Earth Mother, you come back to your true foundation. This place on the Wheel reunites you with your core beliefs about where you came from as an individual and as an integral part of society. Here you see clearly your role in the world and your vision and beliefs about what you can accomplish. At this place on the Wheel, you must challenge your old patterns and belief systems. Some beliefs die hard; they keep coming up so that you can heal at deeper and deeper levels.

Where did you come from? What is your creation myth? What creation teachings did you receive as a child? How do these color your present belief system?

Most indigenous people tell stories of a time when the Earth consisted only of dark water. The story below is based on an Okanagon myth.

In the beginning the Earth was filled with water, and all the creatures lived in the Sky World above the rainbow. It was crowded up there and everyone wondered what lay underneath the water. One brave volunteer—Duck—dived down to retrieve mud from the water's bottom. The mud began to grow, forming land—some say on the back of a great Turtle.

The land was very soft and still, and the animals were anxious to descend from their crowded sky world to earth. The birds ventured out to search for dry land but could find none, so they returned. Finally they sent out Grandfather Buzzard, who flew low over the Earth in search of dry land. He grew tired, and as he flew closer to the Earth, his wings brushed the drying mud and created valleys and mountains.

When the Earth finally dried enough, the creatures came down. They couldn't see very well because there was no sun and moon. They grabbed the sun down from the sky above the rainbow and set it in its track. However, it was too close to the Earth and made everything unbearably hot. Working together, they pushed it farther up into the sky until it was just hot enough.

Then Someone Powerful made the plants and the trees. After making plants and trees, Someone Powerful made men.

As to who retrieved mud from the ocean floor—some say it was Water Beetle, some say Toad, and some say Duck. Some stories recount that the mud was placed on the back of a great Turtle, and some tribes call North America Turtle Island. Other tales detail the origin of the Four Great Winds from the Four Directions.

Many stories include intervention from a higher being who helps create what the creatures need to live on the Earth and, in some cases, instructs people in what to eat and where and how to live. In most of the stories, the people quarrel and the higher being withdraws, leaving humans to fend for themselves on the Earth. These tales are not so different from Old Testament stories or creation accounts from other cultures.

Your beliefs about creation need to be brought into consciousness. According to your core belief system: Where did the Earth come from? Where did people come from? What relationship do people have with the Earth, and what relationship does the Earth have with people? Do the stories you learned in childhood still hold truth for you? What is the relationship between people and animals and plants? What image do you hold of the Creator? Is the Creator male or female, and why? What rules do people have to live by? How do we take care of each other? What are our privileges on this Earth? What are our responsibilities to the Earth and All Our Relations? Do you consider earth, stones, trees and plants, or any other animals to be sentient beings (beings with souls and a free will)? These questions will arise again, later in the chapter.

Earth Mother

When you return to the womb of Earth Mother, you come back to your foundation and your core beliefs about your role in the world—what you envision and what you believe you can accomplish. To understand how the earth, your Mother, can support you, you need to face how your images of Mother facilitate or impede your ability to surrender to her wisdom. Some of us are disconnected from the earth because of circumstances and our urban lifestyle, so we don't remember how to be present with her. Do you trust in her enough to fully ground yourself? Do you believe in your partnership with her enough to accomplish your work?

You may decide that Mother embodies some qualities that are unattractive and unworthy of trust. Experience combined with your internal belief system forms your image of Mother. If you place these qualities or aspects on a Medicine Wheel, you might find the following.

- In the East resides the Mother who has vision. She feeds her children with inspiration, propelling them into the rainbow and beyond. In her negative aspects, she may forget to feed them lunch or to provide adequate boundaries.

- In the South dwells the Mother who raises the crops and tends the animals. She feeds her children corn and beans, nurturing their physical well-being. In her negative aspects, she will demand they be home on time for dinner each and every night, reasonable or not, and will worry incessantly over every bump in their road.

- In the West lives the Mother who is introspective and on a self-healing path. She feeds her children with dreams, giving them the freedom to express heartfelt emotions. In her negative aspects, she is unable to move out of her own self-absorption, sometimes sucking her children into her personal roller-coaster drama.

- In the North resides the Mother who is wise and powerful. She feeds her children with confidence and strength, and has the ability in a single breath to quickly discern what needs to live and what needs to die. In her negative aspects, she may be stuck in her need for recognition and power, and will unmercifully manipulate her children to achieve her own goals.

The Earth Mother can embody all of these aspects, or none of them. She can show any of these faces, depending on which you need to see at the time. She sees all and knows all there is to know about you: every strength and weakness, every tear and every smile. In the center, at the balance point, she is the foundation of all, and holds nothing but unconditional love and incredible acceptance. You may not recognize at any given moment how her love and acceptance manifest, but her love and acceptance are always present.

Path of the White Wolf

Your experience with your human mother, and in some ways with your father, affect what you believe you deserve and what you can accomplish. These beliefs may limit you and you may require healing in order to fulfill your goal and vision. In the Below direction, you must challenge your belief systems. Some beliefs and wounds keep coming up so that you can heal at deeper and deeper levels. You may need many cycles of learning to fully unearth and unravel these issues. Don't get stuck in self-judgment on this. With White Wolf as your witness, just observe, accept, and transform.

Meditation of the Below

Prior to beginning the meditation exercise, use the techniques described in Meditation: Basic Tools in the chapter entitled Preparing for Study, part of the Resources section at the end of the book.

Visualize yourself in harmony with the universe, listen to the slow drum heartbeat of Mother Earth, and use your breath to sink deeper into relaxation and trance. Breathe deeply, consciously relaxing a different part of your body with every breath. Surround yourself with a velvety green moss blanket, knowing that you are protected from any negative energy.

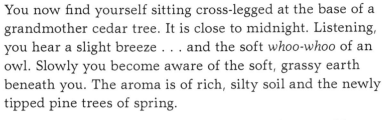

You now find yourself sitting cross-legged at the base of a grandmother cedar tree. It is close to midnight. Listening, you hear a slight breeze . . . and the soft *whoo-whoo* of an owl. Slowly you become aware of the soft, grassy earth beneath you. The aroma is of rich, silty soil and the newly tipped pine trees of spring.

Gradually you notice that you want to lie down and bury your nose in the earth. As you do, your nose is tickled by the touch of a gently yielding mushroom person. So close that you are almost cross-eyed, you observe this mushroom. You sense he has a message for you.

You roll over on your back, reaching out your hand to carefully caress the mushroom. With closed eyes and mind drifting, you wonder what a mushroom could possibly say to you. And then you become aware that the scenery has changed. You are in a cave with a small subterranean pool bubbling up in the middle. There are red and blue people in the cave, and they tell you that they are the mushroom's ancestors.

Leading you to the back of the cave, they disappear into a small opening. The last one beckons you to follow. You hesitate, wondering if you'll even fit, but decide to go. Once you pop through the opening, you find yourself in a very different world. The sky is orange, the plants are purple, indigo, and yellow, and the ground is the color of molten fire. Is this a psychedelic dream? But no, the mushroom people tell you this is the world inside the mother. The rivers run vermilion for they are her blood, the plants are the nutrients that feed her, magma is her core, and her people are the little ones that lived long before man.

As the mushroom man guides you through this world, you stop in awe. The ground beneath you is very hot, and yet you are not burned. Instead, you feel the permeating warmth of the womb. You proceed, ever downward, until you come to the very core of the Earth. You gaze at a fusion of blazing fire, and in its center you see the face of an ancient woman. She smiles at you with radiant love. You sit in her presence, basking in the eternal joy of her tenderness, knowing that she longs to give you your heart's desire.

You know that you can tell her anything with complete confidence that she will support you and help you. You want to share your deepest longings, and somehow you know that she has already understood them without the communication of language. Closing your eyes, you rest, basking in the blissful glow of her affection. *(Drum, medium beat for a minute or so, then increase speed for another minute or so to call the journeyer back.)*

Breathing deeply and peacefully, you begin the journey back to your body in the here and now. When you awaken, you are back on the Earth where you started, with your hand still cupped around your mushroom friend. Slowly, with eyes still closed, you let yourself assimilate your experience. Deliberately, you touch the grass around you, feeling yourself completely grounded. Opening your eyes, you look at the Earth and sky, knowing that you have been in a place where few have ever traveled. You return to your body in the here and now.

Once you open your eyes, write down all that you saw and thought, and begin to work on answering the questions below.

Journal

1. Use your journal to chronicle your journey with your new mushroom friend.

2. List the feelings you experienced in meditation. Write down any new information that was given to you. Review it daily this month, and add to it as you remember more details.

3. List any old beliefs you are holding about the ways in which you are or are not supported in your life. Note the source of each (perhaps your spirit guide gave you this information during the meditation).

Now, ask yourself:

- Do I believe that my dreams can and will manifest?

- Do I know that the invisible world will provide for me on the material plane?

- Can I see how I have been upheld and encouraged along my life path thus far?

- Am I ready to surrender to whatever the universe holds for me?

- Do I have any reservations? List them.

- How might my life be different if I had surrendered to the will of the universe in some other situation?

- Can I see the consequences of holding on to control in my life?

- Can I see the ways I may have limited my possibilities?

- Am I following my life's purpose?

- Am I able to identify my true dreams?

4. Use your journal to record dreams and other visions that you experience during this time. Identify how these supplement or clarify your work with the Below.

5. Define your relationship to the land. What sensations or thoughts does the word *grounded* evoke in you? Describe your relationship to the word *mother*.

6. Assess your ability to be in complete surrender to outside forces, like an infant in the womb. How do you feel about being so vulnerable?

7. Do you currently make room in your life to connect to the Earth? How and when? Do you ground yourself regularly and sit with the Mother to ask her assistance in finding answers to questions or predicaments?

All Our Relations

A Three-Week Written Practice

This exercise involves writing quietly for about 10 to 15 minutes per day for 21 days. You will be writing about earth's creatures or children, your relations from the Seven Directions:

- East, winged ones
- South, four-leggeds
- West, swimming ones
- North, standing ones and plant people
- Above, star beings and two-leggeds
- Below, earth and the mineral kingdom
- Center, those who dwell in spirit, spirit guides, ancestors, angels

Spend three days on each family as follows:

1. Day One: Write whatever comes to mind with regard to your past relationship to each Earth family.

2. Day Two: Read what you wrote on the first day, and ask yourself the questions below as you see these relationships in the present. Build on what you wrote the first day.

   • Are these beings sacred to you? How do you acknowledge them as sacred?

   • Do you use these beings in some way to maintain your own life force, or use products made from any of the beings in this family?

   • How do you care for this Earth family? How do you use your own resources to protect any endangered members of these families or protect habitat needed to maintain wild or natural populations? How are you working to help set aside undeveloped areas of the Earth for the enjoyment of future generations?

3. Day Three: Calling upon your Highest Wisdom, ask how your present relationship to these families could change. Use your opposite hand to record the answers you receive.

At the end of this exercise you will have a much different picture of what it means to be in relationship with the Earth and all Earth families. When you are done with this three-week process, move on to the integration ceremony.

Earth Lodge Ceremony

For a list of tools and general setup instructions, see Basic Tools for Ceremony in the chapter entitled Preparing for Study, part of the Resources section at the end of the book. In addition you will need:

- Portable altar
- Dried lavender and tobacco
- Blanket
- Small paintbrush with some paints or paint pens of your favorite colors, preferably acrylics
- Four special waterproof objects to represent each of the four cardinal directions
- A crystal to represent the Above direction and a representation of your totem animal for the Center direction
- Select a special round flat stone—no larger than the palm of your hand—for the Below or Earth direction. Be sure this stone agrees to be painted as part of this ceremony

This particular ceremony can only be held outside. Find a private place in nature.

- Set protection and establish intention.
- Call in guides and other helpers.
- Begin with your grounding/stillness exercise to establish your connection to the Earth.

Clear a Circle about 8 to 10 feet in diameter. You can build a small lean-to structure with sapling poles if you want a shelter (this is best if you wish to stay overnight). Hunt around for some moss or branches, and use them to create a bed within your Circle. Place a blanket there if you think you'll need one.

Place representative objects at each direction's gateway. Set stones for Father Sky and Mother Earth at the head and foot of the Earth Bed. In the traditional Okanagon way, the head of the bed is in the West, the place of dreams, and the foot in the East, the place of new vision. The stone for the Earth should be fairly round and flat. Place your totem animal representation in the Circle to hold the center.

Bless the objects and stones, smudge with cedar and sage, and call in the Powers of each of the Seven Directions. Call in the relation associated with each direction: East, winged ones; South, four-leggeds; West, swimming ones; North, standing ones and plant people; Above, star beings and two-leggeds; Below, earth and her subterraneans and creepy-crawlers; Center, those who dwell in spirit.

Now enter the Medicine Wheel by the West gate, calling in your totem animals and your ancestors as protectors and guides. Carry the lavender and tobacco, your journal and a pen, and the paint and paintbrush with you. Sit down on the Earth Bed and use the tobacco and lavender to surround yourself with a Circle of protection—just sprinkle the individual herbs around your immediate area.

Next pick up the stone representing the earth and hold it to your heart. Ground yourself and allow your mind to grow silent. Ask the stone what it has to communicate to you. Remember that stones are Earth People, and they carry the records of all that has ever transpired upon this planet. Sit quietly and listen for any messages. Examine the stone carefully; make a connection with it. Ask the stone's permission to decorate it, and allow it to show you the symbols that it wants to show you. Paint it. Let the stone tell you what colors to use.

When the paint has dried, place the stone on your lower abdomen, which is your creative center. Visualize a golden thread running from the crown of your head down through your spine and into the earth at the base of your tailbone. Ask the blessings of the Earth Mother, and that she communicate with you through the golden thread and the stone upon your stomach. As you lie there, feel how the earth supports you, how she nurtures you and accepts you exactly as you are, how she provides for you and all beings who live upon her. Allow your thoughts to drift, and let go into the state of No Mind. It's all right if you go to sleep. Form the conscious intention to remember your dreams.

When you feel complete with this, gently remove the stone, roll over on your stomach, and place the stone on your back just above your tailbone. Now ask the Earth Mother to remove from you anything that keeps you from fulfilling your mission on the Earth. Pray for balance and ask to be shown the things that will help you to balance yourself and the Earth.

Allow your mind to drift into a meditative state or a day-dream, with the purpose of seeing the things you came to this lifetime to accomplish: for yourself, your family, your community, All Your Relations on the Earth, and the world. If you feel you need to release some sadness, it is okay to shed tears. When you finish, gently remove the stone, sit up, and write these things down.

Now just lie on the Earth and enjoy the sensations of sun and sky, fresh air, soft grass and moss, and the ground beneath you. To complete the Earth Lodge Ceremony, think about, and perhaps sing, the song at the end of this section.

Before you leave the Circle, bless and release your ancestors, your totem animals and guides, and the Stone People. Close the Circle by releasing in reverse order each direction you called, and thank each for its support.

Unless you have done this ceremony in a place where you are certain that it won't be disturbed, put everything back in natural order. You can set it up again next time you come.

Song

Everyone has a place,

A place that they call Sacred Space.

Everyone has a place

Deep down inside.

Resting, healing, channeling, feeling,

Loving, nurturing, gently revealing.

Moment to Moment

I am in the moment of breathing the delicious scents of life.
I am in the moment of tasting the sweetness of love.
I am in the moment of hearing a rousing symphony of laughter.
Drinking stars and moon,
Eating wind and sun,
Smelling earth and ocean,
I am in the moment of seeing the face of God in every living thing.
I am in the moment of knowing my essence is immortal.
I am in the moment of sensing there is always beauty and truth
If I but choose to see it.
Thus I can be, moment to moment.

Sandy D'Entremont

Element: *Magic*
Embodiment: *Alchemical*
Emotion: *Detachment*
Season: *NOW*
Time: *Dreamtime*
Moon Cycle: *Blue*
Phase of Life: *Mastery*
Color: *Rainbow*
Creatures: *Those Who Come and Go*
Expression: *Whale Song*
Way: *Weaver of Light*
Place on the Wheel: *Between
    Worlds and Times*
Lesson: *Integrated Connection*
Ceremony: *Awakening the Shield*

Spiraling to the Center

In the Center you find yourself, the integration of all that is. Your Center holds your essence, what some call the higher self or oversoul. This is where you integrate all you have learned on this journey around the Wheel. In this place of magic you can experience complete union—within and without.

In the East you dreamed, then offered your visions to the universe in trust in the South. In the West you released all that stood in the way of manifestation; in the North you called in the knowledge of the past to enlighten your future. Next you invited and invoked the Great Mystery and laid the bundle in the womb of your Mother Earth. Now you are ready to complete the Medicine Bundle you began in the East, to open your bundle of dreams.

All things come to rest in the Center, where you touch the eternal NOW between worlds and times. If you view the Medicine Wheel as a Sacred Hoop with your essential spiritual light at the core, you see the integrated connection of all directions forming an alchemical, rainbow song of pure energy. You can use the tools you've gained and the knowledge from the lessons you've learned in the sacred directions to maintain your balance in the world *and* manifest your dreams.

You've heard the saying "Once in a Blue Moon"? A Blue Moon happens only once every couple of years, and yet once you join in the alchemical process of integration, you live in Blue Moon time, which is ALWAYS and NOW. In Western folklore, the Blue

Moon—the second full moon during a single month of the Gregorian calendar—has become known as a time of power and magic. The spells cast and dreams dreamed culminate in action. And yet there is no such thing as a Blue Moon in indigenous calendars, which are based on a thirteen-moon cycle.

Still, the symbol of the Blue Moon works well because when you live in the Center, *all* possibility is present. You dream, and in weaving your dreams through the web of creation, you manifest your dreams. As you claim the power of living within your Center, you become the adept practitioner of destiny. You create your life. Are you ready to take full responsibility for what you have and are—for what you will give birth to? If you can say a wholehearted "Yes!" you have integrated the lessons on the Wheel.

Whale song is the music of the Center. This gift from another of Earth's sentient beings heals you and can transport you to other realms. As ancient record keepers of Universal Mind, whales remember all that has happened since before they journeyed here. By using the tones that these creatures give us and staying in your Center where time is all happening NOW, you can access knowledge from the age-old chronicles, what some call the akashic records (which we spoke of in the Above Direction), and use them to grow in wisdom.

When you find balance in the Center, you attune yourself to the synchronicity and alchemy of existence on the earth plane. You receive the messages that the Universe or the Great Mystery is sending. Occasionally someone will walk into your life with a message for you and only you, and just as suddenly that person will be gone. This is one of the Creatures Who Come and Go. Christian literature refers to these beings as Angels. Sometimes you will have met a Walk-In, a presence that temporarily occupies a body in order to fulfill a one-time purpose. Once in awhile these beings aren't even human. Now and then an animal totem will take the form of a domestic animal just to whisper in your ear! Has your cat ever shown you something of vital importance? Or maybe a bird appeared out of nowhere, pulling your attention toward something new and interesting?

It is time, now, to review what you have learned in your journey around the Medicine Wheel. For the review, we will use the sacred symbol for infinity—the figure 8—which connects East and West, Illumination and Healing, through the heart. On the Medicine Wheel, this is called the Blue Road of Spirit. It reveals that which is in darkness, in order to transmute pain and confirm healing.

The North and South also connect in the Center, forming within the infinity symbol 8 the Red Road of Physical Reality, where the wisdom of our ancestors joins with the trusting innocence of the child. To stand in integrity and at the same time to possess vulnerability—this is the way of true power.

The Above and Below directions also link with a third infinity symbol. The Above direction holds the information of Universal Consciousness, which is there for you to tap in to at any time. Below is the grounding that unites purpose with passion. When all three infinity symbols link together in a firmly held core, the Wheel's image is that of a multidimensional flower: ever-expanding, growing, blooming. Magic lives at the core, in the Center, and enchantment blossoms.

Extending the teaching further, visualize the horizontal planes of the figure 8 running North to South, with the past behind, the present within, and the future ahead. If you look at it only in the NOW, the horizontal figure 8 represents the relationships that stand behind you in support, as well as the relationships that you are nurturing for the future. The work of intergenerational healing—which most of us require—is to access the pain of the past while staying centered in the present, in order to heal and release future generations from the unconscious, genetic need to repeat the past. To unlock the ancestral wisdom contained within your DNA, you journey from the Center "back" to seek an ancestor guide who will help you to open the gates of wisdom, and then allow that wisdom to flow through you in present-day time. In this way, you can pass it "unto the seventh generation" as the Hopi teaching goes.

As you balance and integrate in the Center, you come full circle. All levels—mental, physical/cellular, emotional, and spiritual—are engaged. Knowledge moves down into the chakras, the energy centers that govern mind, speech, heart, will, creativity, and physical action. Grounded in the physical plane, you can integrate wisdom and understanding with physical action.

As you gain the balance of the Center, you become fully present in each moment. In moving around the Wheel, you have healed part of your past so that it no longer affects your present. Worry over the future is mitigated by your awareness of your responsibility for creating your own reality. You acknowledge that the challenges you face are resplendent with the lessons you chose for this lifetime. You are less attached to your own or others' past or present dramas. You see clearly that all you have is the present moment, and your responsibility is to bring to it your full attention.

Do you know someone, perhaps an elder, who lives fully in his or her power? Most of us do. Reflect for a moment on what you know of his or her life—can you see the integration of the teachings of the Wheel in the way that she presents herself? Your goal is to live in your power, in the Center, like others who have found their way to live fully in their power. Your goal is to become more and more fully present, in order to find the creative ease and expanded perspective that await you.

Welcome to this journey, to this place on the Wheel once again. Welcome to the rainbow healing light, the teaching of movement and integration, and the essence of alchemy. Welcome to the magic and healing that manifest as you tap in to your creative source, the place of dancing and singing to your rhythm, as the Wheel turns in this cycle of learning.

Aho!

Meditation of the Center

Prior to beginning the meditation exercise, use the techniques described in Meditation: Basic Tools in the chapter entitled Preparing for Study, part of the Resources section at the end of the book.

Visualize yourself in harmony with all creation, listen to the slow drum heartbeat of Mother Earth, and use your breath to sink deeper into relaxation and trance. *(Drum for a minute or so.)*

Breathe the brilliant white light of Father Sun into your body, beginning at your crown and traveling down toward your feet. See the light rushing into your body, all of your organs, filling every particle of your being. Consciously relax a specific part of your body with each breath.

Draw the energy of Mother Earth, colored a velvety moss green, up through your feet to your pelvis, up into your solar plexus, heart, throat, third eye, and out through the crown of your head. Feel yourself letting go of all judgment. Become a willing observer. Enjoy the deep primal security and safety of the Mother's gentle embrace. She is the source of manifestation on the physical plane. Let the green light of the Earth Mother flow through you and surround you, caressing you with her love. Then collect both the white and green lights in a pool beneath your feet.

Now visualize indigo: the color of the night sky. Let the indigo light enter through your third eye, sometimes called the Shaman's Eye in the center of your forehead. With the night sky come the stars and the knowledge of the collective consciousness. Let it settle into your body, filtering slowly downward until it flows out the soles of your feet, remaining with the other colors for later use. Be aware of any new thoughts that drift through at this time. If one catches your interest, store it in your memory for future review.

Next comes the clear aqua blue of melting snow water. Allow this soft, clear blue to enter through your throat. This is the color of communication. As the gentle blue light descends tranquilly through your cellular structure, notice any thoughts that enter and any places in your body where it's hard to let the color in. These are the places where the energy of communication is stuck. Concentrate on sensitively pushing the aqua light into these areas. See what thoughts are there. Who and what have you not been addressing in your life that needs to be taken care of? Let the pale turquoise tones stream through your body, running like a bubbling creek out through your feet into the pool of liquid colors.

Moving down to the center of your chest where the breast bones meet, visualize a pale rose pink coloring permeating your heart. As it enters, feel it melt resistance, stubbornness, rebellion, fear, and anger. Allow your heart to open to receive the serene peace of the loving and lovely rose light. As you open in surrender to the rose quartz energy, you may feel a burst of love pour through your being. Allow it to slowly settle in all the pores of your body, cleansing them of toxins and negativity. Then let the crystalline rose light slowly fade out through your pores and into the space around you, collecting with the other colors in the pool at the base of your feet.

Reaching your solar plexus, your base of power, imagine a glowing, golden orange globe of light entering just above your belly. This light is full of energy, and you may feel an instant stimulation from it. This is better than a caffeine high—and it's free! Allow the vitality to course through your bloodstream, flooding your system with power. Notice any places that resist the influx of life force. Ask yourself what your resistance is about, and file the answer for later. Request the golden light to infuse these areas with a rush of energy. When each cell of your body has been bathed in the intensity of the orange-gold light, release it through your feet to join with the other colors there.

Your belly is the Mother of Creativity, the birth place of each infant dream. Pour fiery red-orange light into your belly, feeling it burst into flames of creative action. Allow this light to cleanse you of any feelings of abandonment. Notice whether you feel abandoned by others or yourself, but don't make any judgments. Envision the fire purifying the dark, neglected, and wounded places in your body. Seek the freedom of a new start. Welcome the healing of old, festering injuries. As the fiery reddish light sweeps through your inner cosmos, remember that you are the creator of your dreams, and as such, everything that happens within you is a microcosmic reflection of what you have brought and will bring into being. Know that this is a clean sweep which will allow you to originate new dreams, awash with color and vibrancy. Now send the flaming light down, down through your feet and into the pool of colors.

The colors of the rainbow lie at your feet. Notice which one seems to vibrate the most. Feel its intensity. Hold it in your hands, feel its charge. This is your personal color, and its vibration surrounds you at all times.

Gather all the colors into an ephemeral ball of glowing energy. Hold the ball in your hands, feel it pulsing with vibrant life. Delicately blow on it, dispersing the energy to the four winds, sending it back to the universe to be called in again at will. This is the way that power flows through the dimensional realms, sent wherever it is needed at any given moment. You can call in whatever you need at any time.

Sweetly, in great serenity, sink back to this time and place. *(Drumming changes to a different, faster beat for a minute or so to call the journeyer back.)* Float for awhile on the soft cloud of deep relaxation, no thought, no worries. All is cared for. Know that you *are* the Center of a perfect universe.

Enter your body in the here and now. When you are ready, open your eyes. Hold your hands to your heart and let the essence of your personal color merge with your being. Write down all that you saw and thought, and begin to work on answering the questions on the following pages.

Journal

1. Use your journal to chronicle your impressions of the guided meditation.

2. What colors enticed you the most? Why? What memories do you associate with particular colors? Are they pleasant or unpleasant?

3. Could you sense different energetic vibrations emanating from each color? What did this mean to you? Identify your personal color.

4. What parts of your body resisted the inflow of colors? Did the colors dissolve any of these blocks? Did you receive any healing from this exercise? What did that feel like?

5. Record any thoughts associated with any of the resistances in your body. Did you gain any new insights as to where your personal wounds reside and what you can do to heal them?

6. Did you receive any new information from the Universal Mind? Record it here.

7. Were there any obstructions in your communication center? Did you identify anyone that you need to clear up old issues with? Are you ready to do this?

8. Did you find in your body any impediments to receiving love in the form of the crystal rose light? Where? Do you have any memories associated with it? Are you ready to let them go?

9. Were you able to receive the orange globe of power? If not, why not? If you were, and this is a new feeling for you, describe it in detail.

10. Did you notice any place in your body where your creative instincts are shut down? If so, why? Do you understand the cause? Write about it.

11. Take some time to research the different energy centers, or chakras, in your body.

12. Set aside some time to reconnect with universal mind while listening to whale song this month. You can find whale song on CD, or even on the Internet.

Integrating Within: Aspects in Summary

The lesson of the Center direction is integrated connection. To experience integrated connection, you must complete the spiral and assimilate your experiences. You have learned a great deal about the Medicine Wheel and yourself. You have traveled the Spiral Path with White Wolf, explored aspects of the Wheel, journeyed in meditation to discover sacred and important information, and noted how the teachings affect your three-dimensional reality through inquiry and written exercises.

Below are summarized the aspects of each direction so that you can view the Wheel as a whole and begin this final lesson: movement on the Wheel.

Movement on the Wheel entails living what you have learned and bringing this wisdom into your daily life. It is challenging to remember metaphysical teachings when coping with the 60-mile-per-second technical world we inhabit. It takes your full presence and conscious practice to observe yourself without judgment as you integrate this knowledge into your life.

Throughout this book, you have worked on four levels: spiritual, physical, emotional, and mental. You now know that learning and change take place when all levels are engaged. We humans are both creators and destroyers: every day, in every moment. Often when we bring something

Aspect	East	South	West	North	Above	Below	Center
Element	Air	Fire	Water	Stone	Space	Organic	Magic
Emotion	Excitement	Passion	Grief/Joy	Serenity/Gratitude	Emptiness	Acceptance	Detachment
Embodiment	Spiritual	Physical	Emotional	Mental	Ethereal	Source	Alchemical
Season	Spring	Summer	Autumn	Winter	Eternal	Yearly	NOW
Time	Dawn	Noon	Dusk	Night	Timeless	Midnight	Dreamtime
Moon	Waxing	Full	Waning	New	Void of Course	Dark	Blue
Phase	No Form	Youth	Mature	Elder	Perpetual	Inception	Mastery
Color	Yellow	Red	Black	White	Indigo	Moss Green	Rainbow
Creature	Winged Ones	Four-legged	Swimmers	Standing ones	Star People	Subterraneans	Those Who Come & Go
Expression	Breath	Drum	Water	Rattle	Toning	Tears	Whale Song
Way	Seeker of Vision	Creator of Movement	Mirror	Mentor	Union with Void	Birth and Rebirth	Weaver of Light
Place	Inspiration	Growth	Balance	Truth	Openness	Initiation	Between Worlds
Lesson	Awareness/Illumination	Trust/Innocence	Introspection/Dreaming	Wisdom/Power	Universal Consciousness	Pregnancy Possibility	Integrated Connection
Ceremony	Calling Home	Dance	Cleansing	Prayer	Star Wheel	Earth Lodge	Shield

from imagination to the earth plane (three-dimensional reality) our creation is not what we expect, or we ignore what we've created and abandon responsibility for it.

With this in mind, let's revisit the basic steps of manifestation.

- Inspiration: When ideas come into your consciousness.
- Intention: Identifying and clarifying your vision/desire.
- Calling: Visualization or guided meditation to open to possibility and to additional information from spirit.
- Passionate purpose: Connecting with your heart's desire, integrity, and caring.
- Disciplined application: Deeper exploration through inquiry, observation of your world, and commitment to your work.
- Creation: Birthing your desires in the world.
- Initiation: The first physical manifestation combines your experience with your understanding of your creation.

Perfecting this process *and* allowing room for spirit to improvise on your behalf is a lifelong endeavor. Improvement and mastery take practice. As you take each step in the process, you must acknowledge the result of your spiritual work. The result will present itself to you in three-dimensional reality. Spiritual teachings and truths are not just in your head or in your dreams or in your heart; you continually manifest/create/destroy in three-dimensional reality. In this way, you mirror back to yourself your own unique belief system.

Recently, a friend of ours prepared humbly and diligently for a Buddhist ceremony at which she planned to take vows. She had been on a spiritual path for a number of years and studied hard. This was a momentous occasion in her life. She attended the ceremony, and afterward began the drive home with great happiness. As she approached a local ice cream shop, she decided to stop and treat herself. At that moment someone drove in front of her, cutting her off, nearly sideswiping her truck. Heart pounding, she slammed on her brakes. The words that came to her mind were *not* particularly spiritual. The teaching was in her ability to note her response, practice detachment without judgment, and laugh about it later as a lesson on her road.

In some ways, our twenty-first-century challenge is greater than that of our ancestors. Few of us have the luxury of sequestering ourselves in the wilderness to discover deeper levels of spirituality for any extended period of time. We have no choice but to work within the construct of earth-plane reality: subways, highways, Internet, media, offices, and telephones included. Life gets very full as we deal with the information coming at us from all sides. Work commitments, bills to pay, and relationships can take up the best part of every 24 hours. It is easy to separate spiritual work from physical reality, and neglect the final steps of integration.

The exercise/ceremony in this section will deepen your understanding of the synergistic aspects of the Wheel and work with your physical body to bring the cycle of learning full circle. Remember: balancing in the Center is the key; movement around the Wheel brings the teaching full circle.

Be sure to read the exercise/ceremony a few times before actually doing it.

Ceremony:
Dancing and Chanting the Wheel

A Three-Week Practice

Focused intention creates manifestation. As you walk the Medicine Path with White Wolf, consciously work to incorporate your new beliefs into your body. This will ground your intention and bring knowledge more completely into your physical being. One of the best ways to do this is to create your own Medicine Wheel dance and song, which will be your primary work this month.

Choose a location. For a list of tools and general setup instructions, see Basic Tools for Ceremony in the chapter entitled Preparing for Study, part of the Resources section at the end of the book. In addition you will need some water and fruit or another snack for break time.

Begin by creating a Circle, preferably outside, or in an uncluttered interior space. Purify the area by smudging with sage. Then sanctify it by smudging for healing with cedar. Start with the sage in the east, smudging in a sunwise (clockwise) circle about 6 to 10 feet in diameter.

Call in the Powers of each Direction for protection: Visionary Eagle of Illumination sits in the East, Protective Rattlesnake of Trust in the South, Healing Bear of Introspection in the West, and Wise Buffalo of Knowledge sits in the North. Call in the aspects of each of these four directions, and place the sacred object you brought to represent the direction at the Circle's perimeter. Take a few moments to feel the essence of what the direction means to you, what strengths and wisdom the direction represents as it is called into your Circle. Acknowledge the presence of White Wolf.

After using the sage, smudge in a moonwise (counter-clockwise) motion with the cedar, asking the Powers of Father Sky, Mother

Earth, and your higher self to help you release all that no longer serves you. Again, call in the aspects of each Center Direction. Place the sacred objects for the Center in the middle of your Circle, with space left for you to sit in the center.

As you feel the essence of each sacred direction—the strengths and wisdom each represents as it is called into your Circle—call in the strength and wisdom of White Wolf to sit with you in the Center and guide you.

For a few moments sit with your back to the South. Look at, or visualize with your eyes closed, the object you have brought to represent each direction. Think about the aspects of each direction as you have called them in. Take a few moments to feel the essence of each direction as it works within the whole Wheel: the role it plays, the strengths it brings, the wisdom it holds.

Think about how the Wheel works as a unified whole.

- Vision and illumination enter the Wheel in the East.
- Growth, blossoming, and movement in trust, innocence, and love exist in the South.
- Balance, analysis, and maturity through introspection reside in the West.
- Deepening of wisdom and power in truth take place in the North.
- Openness and connection with the Great Mystery abide in the void Above.
- Grounding and release in surrender to the source reside Below.
- Manifestation and serendipitous alchemy resonate in the NOW.

Although you may not be able to identify who, what, when, and how for each step, that's okay. Each cycle of learning takes a different path, depending on the individual and on the process or situation. It is enough to know that the Wheel exists for you as a tool, and that you are on the path to understanding how it works. With practice, it gets easier.

Now leave the Wheel, turn on your drumming tape or CD, and reenter by the East gate. Standing at the Center, listen to the heartbeat of the drums. Relax your body by stretching: Reach your hands down to touch the earth, drawing her clear moss green energy upward through your chakras and out through the crown of your head. Reach your hands to the sky, pulling down the white-gold light of illumination through your crown, sending it all the way through your body and out through your feet. Visualize the twin flames of the Earth Mother and Sky Father melting together in union in your heart.

Now begin to quietly hum or sound a tone that comes purely from your heart.

At the same time, let your body begin to move to the rhythm of the drums. Don't push yourself into a known dance, but rather allow yourself to feel your internal dance. As your body begins to move, visualize the beliefs you want to release. Feel your power and the emotions evoked. Dance them. Sing them. Let your body and your song lead you. Use words if you want to, but vocables *(ah, ee, eh, oh)* often work even better. Remember that you are in charge of your emotions and of creating beliefs. Allow your movement to be gentle but powerful.

Dance for five to ten minutes circling the Wheel, then step out of the Circle by the West gate, thanking the Great Bear, the totem for West, for her healing. Rest for a time. Drink some water. Acknowledge the power in pure creation.

Now step into the Wheel at the South Gate. Here you enter with the trust of a child, asking for the power of your new beliefs to manifest in your life. Repeat the exercise of visualizing the twin colored flames from Earth and Sky dancing in your heart.

Begin to hum or tone, and allow your voice to express your new beliefs. Feel the drum heartbeats. Let yourself begin to flow with the pulse of your new beliefs. Feel the joy of release and transformation, and evoke it in your dance and song. Picture the way your life will look after you incorporate these new pathways. Know that you are creating cellular memories that will flow over the old pathways in your spirit, mind, emotions, and body—new patterns that will erase the old.

Dance for five to ten minutes circling the Wheel, then leave the Circle by the North gate, thanking Buffalo, the totem of North, for sacrificing your old beliefs to the wisdom of the new yet ancient knowledge you have gained. Rest for a time. Drink some water. Eat some fruit. Acknowledge again the power of new creation.

Now visualize the Medicine Wheel as a sphere with three intersecting figure 8s (the symbol for infinity), two horizontal and one vertical, with your body as the connecting center. The 8 that links the East and West, Illumination and Healing, through the heart is the Blue Road of Spirit, which teaches you to shed light on that which is in darkness in order to transmute pain and confirm healing.

The second horizontal figure 8, North and South, also connects in your center as the Red Road of Physical Reality. On this path you unite the wisdom of your ancestors with the trusting innocence of the child. This is the way of true power—to stand in integrity and to be vulnerable. The vertical figure 8 is the sustenance you receive from Above and Below, the twin flames in your heart that you visualized earlier.

Step into the Wheel again, and dance the infinity symbols East to West, North to South, with your arms high for Above and touching the Earth for Below. Feel the movement of these different energies through your body. Picture how the Wheel supports you and teaches you.

Dance for five to ten minutes, then leave the Circle by the East gate, thanking all of the directions for their protection and wisdom. Release the directions from the Circle and pick up the sacred objects you brought to represent the directions.

Now, consider the following questions.

1. What pictures do you see? What songs came forth in this Movement Ceremony?
2. What dance does your body enjoy expressing? How does it feel for your physical body to incorporate your new beliefs?

3. What old beliefs and patterns were you aware of releasing during the dance exercise? What new beliefs are you bringing into your life? Are you surprised?

Dance and sing the Wheel at least every few days this month. Notice how your dance and chant changes as your old beliefs transform. Perhaps a poem will emerge during this time, and a choreography that feels cohesive. Be sure to pay close attention to the things that happen in your everyday life, and try to determine without judgment or attachment how you participated in creating these events in your reality. Then let it all go.

Path of the White Wolf

When you have completed this dance a few times, you will be ready to create your personal shield.

Creating a Medicine Shield

This month you will create a Medicine Shield to help you integrate what you have learned on your walk around the Medicine Wheel.

This is the Center Shield for the Seven Sacred Directions, and you may find it integrates symbols, colors, and images from all of the directions. In general, your Shield should be made in a round shape and incorporate the quadrants of the Medicine Wheel. You may draw your Shield with colored pencils, pen and ink, or paints—or any media you choose. Or you can craft your Shield from a wooden hoop with rawhide stretched inside, using feathers and bones and other natural treasures for decoration.

Don't worry if you feel that you lack artistic ability. Your Shield can be very simple.

1. If you want to draw your Shield, start by drawing a circle about the size of a dinner plate or a little larger. Place your hands (one at a time) in line with the quarter-sections on the circle. Trace your hands: right hand in the East, left in the West, right in the North, left in the South. Then color these representations in the colors of the directions.

2. Next, on the right side of your Shield, create a section to represent your experience of the East, Illumination. Add symbols, drawings, colors, and shapes that depict what you learned about yourself when you worked with the material in that chapter, and how the lesson of Illumination increased your Vision.

3. Continue around the Circle, letting your symbols reflect what you learned in each quadrant: Trust in the South, Healing in the West, Wisdom in the North. In the middle of the Shield, put images or drawings symbolizing your work with the Above, Below, and Center directions.

Call in the strength and wisdom of White Wolf to be with you while you create this powerful tool.

You may want to draw with your non-dominant hand. Like the writing exercise for the Above direction, this kinesthetically challenging exercise opens your creative mind. And, if your creativity prompts you to make a Shield different from the model suggested above, follow that impulse. Move with the spirit of your own creative force. There is no right or wrong Center Shield.

Your Shield may be as simple or complex as you want to make it. It will be a lasting record of your first journey around the Wheel. Allow yourself to express what you feel, let your Shield proclaim your freedom and power, and above all, your joy!

Shield Awakening Ceremony

This is a Shield Ceremony. Prepare by using the same area and format you used in the Dancing and Chanting the Wheel exercise earlier in this chapter.

- Bring your drum or rattle.
- Bring your Center Shield.
- Bring a staff to be placed into the ground in the middle of the Medicine Wheel (or other alternative if doing this ceremony indoors).

After you prepare the Circle, stand in the center of the Wheel and raise your Center Shield above your head. Call in the powers and colors of each cardinal direction, starting with the East. Offer your Center Shield toward each directional gate as you call forth the aspects of the directions. Acknowledge and give thanks for the lessons you have learned through each doorway. Be specific and take your time. It is important to tell the Spirit World what you have received. Ask the ancestors and the powers in your Shield to be your guides and protectors.

After you call in the cardinal directions, place a representation of Above and Below in the middle of the Wheel and call in these directions.

Next, place your staff into the ground at the halfway point between the representations of Above and Below. Stand again in the Center, raise your Center Shield above your head, and call in the Above and Below directions.

As you call in the Center direction, bring your Shield down to heart level. Welcome your totem animals and spirit helpers, your color, song, and dance. Call in the teacher-guide White Wolf to stand with you in the center of the Spiral Path. Tie your Center Shield to the staff.

Turn on your drumming tape or CD and, using your drum and rattle, complete the dance/chant exercise you have practiced on numerous occasions this month. Honor yourself, the Seven Directions, and your Center Shield as you complete this ritual one last time. As you dance, ask the essence of each symbol on your Shield to enter it and awaken its power.

When you are finished, take your Shield down from the center staff and sit for awhile in the Circle holding the shield in your lap, or lie down and place it on your chest. Feel the power of your Medicine Shield. Visualize the Spiral Path you have traveled. Feel the camaraderie of White Wolf as you remain in the Center.

Close the Circle by releasing each direction you called to partake of the ceremony, and thank each one for its support. You have now awakened your Medicine Shield. Know it is charged with the Powers with which you have been working, and that it will provide you with blessings and protection. Use the Shield as a tangible reminder of the teachings. You can hang your Seven Directions Medicine Shield in a special location, perhaps above your altar.

Taking Pause

So, you've traveled the Spiral Path, journeyed around the Wheel and into the Center.

What's next?

You may want to rest now, to stop the intensity of learning, return to "real life," relax into more normal pursuits. Or you may want to press ahead and fill yourself with new teachings. Before switching gears entirely, we ask that you take some integration time.

You need time to rest and reflect. Indigenous peoples recognize rest to be an intrinsic step in understanding messages from the spirit world. For the Sun Dance Ceremony of the North American Plains tribes, participants withdraw from worldly pursuits four days before the ceremony and four days after. Robin tells of the time she insisted on returning to a corporate job a few days after Sun Dance. She was still half in and half out of the Spirit World. The simple act of driving a car was a challenge. On her way home, she had to stop and sleep for several hours. Unloading the car presented no problem at all: she put her wallet in the refrigerator and the bacon in the cupboard! (Luckily, her daughter found them both and put them where they belonged.)

Without a pause, renewal can't take place. Substituting action for reflection draws your attention away from the power of your experiences. As the Christian Bible tells us, on the seventh day God rested. There needs to be balance and time to allow the teachings to percolate so that a deeper understanding can arise.

Now is the time to gather strength for the next task or teaching. Allow yourself to rest and become filled with energy, love, and strength so that you can GiveAway again.

As you integrate your experiences, you can begin to practice what you have learned on the Path of the White Wolf, and open to the messages and teachings all around you. Spirit is always with you, if you take the time to see it.

As part of this resting time, we invite you to honor and celebrate your journey and to GiveAway to yourself by holding your own Life Transition Ceremony.

Your Own Ceremony

Ceremony unites group members and celebrates accomplishments and transitional milestones. During your journey on this path, you performed ceremonies for yourself to help you integrate and honor the teachings. Although details in each ceremony differ slightly, the format by now is familiar to you.

To mark the completion of this spiral of learning you will now create a ceremony that is uniquely your own. This final lesson can take many forms, but regardless of form or choice, it is meant to focus on your personal transformation. For a list of tools and general setup instructions, see Basic Tools for Ceremony in the chapter entitled Preparing for Study, part of the Resources section at the end of the book.

Ceremony Planning

1. Take time to look back over the path you've traveled. Think about where you were before you started this spiral of learning—the challenges you were dealing with, your understanding of self, your life situation. This may be a good time to write a review in your journal, even if it's a simple list of Before and Now observations. You'll be able to refer to the list in the future, and it will help you see how you've continued to grow over time.

2. Review your personal vision, recorded in the "Ultimate Man or Woman" essay that you completed in the East. Think about your journey and the exercises in each direction: consider your power animal from the South, those you needed to forgive in the West, your ancestors and authentic self in the North, the experience of opening to Above and surrendering to Below. How did all that bring you to NOW? Congratulate yourself on your accomplishments!

3. Call in your teachers, guides, animal totem, and the White Wolf for council. Ask them what form your ceremony should take. Meditate on what would best meet your needs.

4. Identify the ceremony format that's right for you. Review the Sacred Elements section and re-read the information on Life Transition and GiveAway, Sweat Lodge, Pipe, Making Right Circle, Prayer Ties, and Moon Lodge (for women). Depending on your situation and needs, your ceremony will undoubtedly incorporate one or more of these elements.

5. Go out into your community and locate someone with experience in the type of ceremony you want to conduct. Discuss your situation, needs, and wants with this person, and ask him to help you with creating and performing your ceremony. Do not expect to retain control over all parts of the ceremony. The facilitator will have his own way of doing things, according to the way he was taught. This will be a learning experience for you as you observe the way in which the facilitator goes about his business. (For example, if you ask someone to pour a Sweat Lodge or conduct a Pipe Ceremony, you would not tell him what prayers to pray or what songs to sing.) Discuss what you think you'd like to see in the ceremony, but do not get attached to details. Follow the direction of the facilitator with respect.

If you cannot locate an experienced facilitator, we encourage you to plan your own simplified ceremony based on those referenced in this book—particularly the Life Transition and GiveAway ceremonies. After all, this *is* a rite of passage! You know how to Call the Circle—so call your friends, create the Medicine Wheel together, and assign

Path of the White Wolf

each friend a task (a prayer, a poem, prayer ties, smudging, singing, and so on). Call on the power of community to help you celebrate.

6. Select a day and time for your ceremony, being aware that many events work on "spirit time"—they start when they start and end when they end (make sure any other attendees understand this too). Making plans before or after the ceremony is not recommended (but some of us have to learn that lesson through experience).

7. For ceremony participants select people close to you, with whom you want to share this event and witness your accomplishment. Choose those who are supportive of this path and will be able to share your joy. Work with the facilitator to identify whether there are particular tasks you want them to do for you, such as calling directions, saying prayers, smudging, and other ceremonial practices. Discuss the format with the participants and tell them what to bring if they don't already know.

8. Decide on the best way to gift the facilitator, the facilitator's assistant, and the ceremony participants who came to support you. See the section entitled "A Word About Gifting," which follows.

9. Have a wonderful ceremony day!

We cannot stress how important witnesses are as a part of this process. Those who participate in your ceremony as witnesses not only acknowledge your accomplishments in the moment, but they can also help you remember your achievements when you feel discouraged. We all encounter moments in life when we need help remembering how much we've grown and changed!

A Word About Gifting

Anytime you give or receive goods or services, an energy exchange occurs. If the dynamic, energetic balance of giving and receiving is not maintained in one area of your life, other areas will fall out of synch. Through gifting your facilitator and those who support you in your ceremony, you not only show appreciation for their work and acknowledge their contribution to your growth, but you also maintain energetic balance.

Some facilitators will tell you in the beginning what they expect to receive—not always money—and others will leave it up to you. Either way, the ceremony is not complete without gifting.

If you aren't able to give money, that's okay. There are other ways to gift people who offer you spiritual teaching. Balancing energy exchange, or bartering, is an excellent alternative to a financial gift, especially if funds are in short supply. Ancients conducted all their business through bartering. A farmer traded chickens for herbal remedies from the local healer, for example. In modern times currency replaces bartering, but currency is also an energy exchange. As one of Robin's teachers quipped, "It's called *currency* for a reason! It's a current of energy, just like electricity. And just like any other current, it needs to flow. When one stops the flow, one is unable to fully receive what's been given." Money/currency is energy exchange, and it, too, can get out of balance.

In many native circles, gifting takes the form of tobacco, which symbolizes respect for the teacher's wisdom. Of course, as a many medicine people will tell you, "Tobacco does not pay the rent or the telephone bill." Hint: it's probably okay to include a monetary donation with the tobacco. You may also place a donation basket in a convenient place so that participants can offer money, particularly if the facilitator incurred travel expenses.

Tithing is another form of balancing energy exchange. It is a traditional Christian concept and practice that involves giving a percentage of income to the church. We encourage you to think about it a different way, however. Keep your energy exchange dynamic in balance by tithing appropriately *to the source that nurtures you spiritually*—whatever that source is: the Earth, yourself, a medicine teacher.

If you decide not to give money, gifts can be simple, like a crystal or other stone, sage or other herb, a book, or a beautiful plant. More elaborate gifts such as drums, rattles, jewelry, baskets, or beadwork are entirely appropriate.

If your ceremony will include other forms of GiveAway—either from you to the participants or from participants to you (both are optional but make for a special remembrance of the day), discuss this with the participants so there are no misunderstandings.

On to the Next Adventure

You now stand at the threshold of your next adventure on your spiritual path. As we said in the beginning, the Path of the White Wolf is circular, revolutionary, taking you deeper when you are ready. Consider the image of a helix: each revolution of the path brings you back to the same place on the spiral, but at a slightly higher level. We cycle the Wheel again and again as we evolve, learning something new each time.

As your next cycle of learning begins—whatever it might be—you now possess a deeper understanding of how to use the Medicine Wheel's principles. As you embark on this cycle, you will see, with your vision in the East, that you incorporate the elements of trust and work in the South, and that the North's wisdom becomes more meaningful when blended with healing work in the West. When you complete the cycle, pulling it deep within yourself, you'll recognize the need to connect to inspiration Above/Great Mystery, to ground Below/Earth Mother, and to honor integration in the Center/Within. You'll stand fully present in the balanced Center, holding tremendous power.

Several years ago, after making a life-changing decision and taking pause to get a massage, Robin received a vision.

First I saw myself walking through a mountain meadow in the snow. I was dressed in a beaded white doeskin dress with knee-high white moccasins and a fur-lined white buffalo parka. My friend Nahani, a White Wolf, led me across the meadow. Suddenly, a huge White Bear loomed over me. It wasn't aggressive; rather, it stood in a protective stance. After a few seconds both Bear and

Wolf morphed into mountains, and I found myself standing between them. At that moment, a White Raven flew over me and soared through the pass between the mountains. The White Raven told me, "Go to where the White Wolf and the White Bear meet."

Much later I found out that there are two areas in North America where the White Wolf and the White Bear both lived. The Tsalagi (Cherokee), who lived in the Great Smoky Mountains, knew and held sacred both the White Grizzly Bear and the White Wolf. And the origin of the Okanagan River in Canada is one of the few places in the world where the White Spirit Bear—the Kermode—is known to reside. (Kermode is a subspecies of black bear. A recessive gene in both parents makes the black bear white. It's possible for a family to have white and black bear cubs at the same time!) And of course White Wolves have lived in the area for centuries as well.

Isn't it amazing that this vision would point me to the origin of both my parental lineages?

In Robin's story, her teacher, White Wolf, led her to this information. In the same way, your own spirit animal allies or ancestors may lead you to a glimpse of what is next for you!

Circling and Cycling

To move into the next cycle, peer into the wilderness of your heart's desire and envision what it will be. Define your intention. You may feel a yearning to explore some aspects of Earth-based spirituality or shamanism more fully. While you have barely scratched the surface of these subjects in this book, you have a foundation that will serve you as you move forward. Entire universes of teachings and a lifetime of learning await you.

You may explore many traditions on this path. There are a number of fine teachers who have stepped forward to share their wisdom. We encourage you to find a local spiritual community, which will help you go even deeper into medicine work.

Your decisions, priorities, and experiences determine where you go, what you do, what you learn, who you meet—and spirit has its own hand in some of that, too. How high and deep you go is entirely up to you. If this way is not for you, there are many other strong spiritual paths to explore. There is no right or wrong here, only choices, including the choice to rest from continuing any active spiritual work. Wherever you are on the path is where you belong.

Whatever choices you consider, know that your ancestors, totem animals, spirit teachers, and White Wolf will help orient you. It's interesting how this works. If you take a few steps in a clear direction that supports your highest purpose and All Your Relations, the universe will often do the rest of the work for you. Things will fall into place in a manner both synchronistic and synergetic. People will enter and/or leave your life as if by design. Offers and opportunities may suddenly appear from the most unlikely sources. Your dreams may provide answers to age-old dilemmas. And you will continue to encounter the lessons you need for your personal spiritual evolution, regardless of whether or not you are actively pursuing any particular teaching. After all, wherever you go, you're the first one you meet.

You will undoubtedly feel overwhelmed at times. You may be uncertain as to right action. When this occurs, yield to the universe flowing around you. Be willing to experience life as it is, and take responsibility for what happens. You have the ability to choose your response to situations. Practice detachment from outcome. Pray, meditate, and find your center, where all is in balance. Remember that you create your own reality; your internal struggles are mirrored in what you see around you. If something is happening that you don't like, look for the gift, the lesson, the mirror.

Make the decisions you need to make with careful thought, asking yourself whether each decision supports your highest good and the good of All Your Relations. Call on the wisdom of White Wolf, on your power animals and spirit teachers: ask them to accompany you when you need help with something . . . or when you just need a friend. Listen to the wild instincts in yourself.

Now is a good time to reflect on inward changes to see how they apply in the outer world. Is it time for a new job? A new way of presenting yourself to friends, family, colleagues? Perhaps you will find that you care about Mother Earth and All Your Relations in such a new and different way that you want to research what you can do to assist world change. Although it is rare that one person single-handedly changes the world, by shifting our priorities and ourselves, we become the example that elicits change in others. This is called the Power of One.

Path of the White Wolf

Carlos Castaneda spoke of "changing our assemblage point," the point of balance within each one of us. Once you've changed your ability to maintain balance through inner work, the world around you begins to change with you. And so it is throughout the dance of life. . .

Techqua Ikachi! Blend with Mother Earth and celebrate life!

As you step forward, remember to thank the Great Mystery for the wonder and beauty in the world. Trust that all of your life lessons and experiences are for your highest good and have been planned before your birth. Thank All Your Relations for the opportunity to continue learning on our beautiful planet, Mother Earth.

Gaze into the eyes of White Wolf and know that there is always a place for you.

Look at your Medicine Shield and re-member who you are.

Aho Mitakuye Oyasin! All Our Relations!

Resources

Preparing for Study

The way in which you prepare for any situation—be it a journey, a relationship, or a phase of life—is significant. The more conscious you are as you prepare, the more likely you are to be successful in your endeavor.

Preparation for setting foot on the Path of the White Wolf includes gathering some tools that will support your personal work and help you on the way. Approach your gathering preparation as a sacred act that connects you to the ageless wisdom of the White Wolf. You will refer back to this section often, especially in the beginning.

Setting Intention

Clarifying intention is sometimes the hardest part of finding our way in the world, because we resist taking the time to slow down and identify what we really want in a particular situation or relationship. But a clear intention will smooth your way.

Whether your current intention is world peace, harmonious relations, personal healing, or success, define what it means to you. Think about what you want to accomplish and what you most need to know to take the next steps. Ground your intention in the here and now by thinking about what you can do today, this week, this month, to support your intention. You can view intention as a giving and receiving quotient: what do I have to give, what would I like to receive? Or, what do I need to release, what would I like to bring into my life?

Leave room for spirit to improvise, and keep your intention simple. For example, if you set an intention with intricate detail, you may limit your experience. We find it useful to remind ourselves "This, or something better," and are often pleasantly surprised at the outcome.

Bear in mind that thoughts *are* things. Karmic law provides that what you give out will return to you tenfold. Remember to affirm "harm to none."

Prayer and Meditation

We communicate with spirit—the Creator, Great Mystery, or whatever you choose to call the divine—through prayer and meditation. In prayer we talk to our divine source. In meditation we listen as we empty ourselves of thought to receive inspiration.

All prayer takes is speaking from your heart. You don't need to speak in elaborate verse or use some ancient formula to pray. It's just you and the Great Mystery—speak honestly what you feel and think. Simple prayers like "Thank you" and "Please help me" are sometimes the most powerful. Turn over your worries in prayer. Release your concerns to spirit.

You can offer prayers of gratitude for the blessings you have in your life, as well as prayers for yourself, loved ones, community, the world, and the Earth. You can never pray too much; in these times your prayers are sorely needed.

In meditation you relax and empty your mind of conscious, distracting thoughts and images. It is often impossible to completely still the mind, especially at the beginning. So practice simply watching thoughts flow through, like clouds in the sky, and you will find yourself detaching from mental turmoil and confusion. Meditation clears the way for receiving messages from spirit, your higher self, or guides—especially when used in conjunction with visualization and journeying (see below). A regular meditation practice deepens your connection to the creative source and rejuvenates your energy field. Meditation can also help you release earthly attachments and move toward enlightenment.

Meditation: Basic Tools

- Journal
- Seven Sacred Meditations CD designed to accompany this book *(sold separately)*; CD player
- Cedar and sage smudge
- Candles, matches

Preparing for Meditation

- Cue up your CD player to the meditation appropriate for the direction. If you are doing the meditation in a group, assign someone to turn the CD on and off, if needed, or have someone read the meditation out loud, maintaining a gentle heartbeat rhythm on a drum to ground you.
- Set Sacred Space.
- Smudge for clearing and cleansing.
- Ground yourself: establish your connection to the Earth.
- Review your intention.
- Call in the circle; say a prayer for protection.
- Call in the directions. Light the altar candles, if you are using them.
- Request the presence of guides and other helpers.
- Turn on the CD and begin the meditation.

Creating Sacred Space

Work of the spirit requires space that is harmonious, clean, and quiet. The proper environment is essential to maintain focus and support transformation. This space can be a small corner of your apartment or home—any space that you consecrate to your personal work will support, nourish, and protect you.

In your private sacred space you will set up an altar, store your workbook and journal, meditate, pray, write, and perform other practices. For some of this work you need uninterrupted privacy, so make agreements with those you live with to provide yourself the quiet, alone time you need.

We also recommend that you set aside special, comfortable clothes to wear in your sacred space and for your practices of meditation, visualization, and ceremony.

In addition to your indoor space, find some outdoor spaces that feel good to you—places where you feel welcome and safe, where you have some level of privacy, and where you sense a strong connection with nature.

Altars

For as long as human beings have been on this Earth, we have created altars of one kind or another. Also called "faces of the Earth," on this path they symbolize aspects of the Great Mystery. We create these sacred shrines for specific reasons, for example, to honor a sacred place or a particular person, or for prayer and meditation.

If you do not already have a personal altar, we recommend that you create one for your medicine work. It can be as simple as a small table adorned with a beautiful cloth, or as elaborate as a temple.

On your altar, place representations of each of the seven directions. The altar's size is not important, but you'll want to have enough space to include all the aspects we discuss in this book.

East – air, spring, yellow, dawn, awareness and illumination, eagle

South – fire, summer, red, day, trust and innocence, coyote

West – water, fall, black, dusk, introspection and dreaming, bear

North – stones, winter, white, night, ancestral wisdom and power, buffalo

Above – space, eternal, indigo, timeless, universal consciousness, star people

Below – organic, yearly, moss green, midnight, pregnancy of possibility, subterraneans

Center – magic, now, rainbow, dreamtime, integrated connection, Those Who Come and Go (guides and helpers)

Your altar will become a work of sacred art as you add objects and symbols that you love and find beautiful and that have meaning for you. You may change the altar with the seasons or with the work you do: it will reflect your inner journey. You may want to light a colored candle for each cardinal direction when you meditate or do other inner work. Allow your creativity to flow, and may your altar be a place of light and healing.

Calling the Circle

As you call upon the Great Mystery, your entire being opens up and all of your senses become more alive and more sensitive to the ebbs and flows of energies within yourself and outside of yourself. In the beginning this experience may be uncomfortable and, at times, a little scary. Your refuge is your sacred space, which can be protected by using special methods that cleanse and seal its energy.

We use several techniques to do this. Primarily we use smudging, which is detailed below, and Calling a Circle.

Smudging

Smudging is the ritual cleansing of an object, an energy field, or area such as a room. You also smudge yourself to prepare for inner work or ceremony. The most common smudging technique is to use the smoke from herbs like sage, cedar, or sweetgrass. Burn loose herbs in a fired earthen bowl or a shell, or as a tied bundle, called a smudge stick. The herb's smoke cleanses your energy field as it touches your front torso, your backside, the soles of your

Basic Tools for Ceremony

Ceremonial Objects

Check your local bookstore, gift shop, or music store—or even Internet sources—to locate these items.

- Items needed to create your altar, which are detailed for each ceremony.
- Smudge: Different types of herbs for different ceremonies and purposes.
- Colored candles, any size; tealights work well.
- Matches or lighter.
- Journal.
- Drumming tape (for certain ceremonies).
- Drum (optional).
- Rattle: Can be as simple as dried beans or small beads in any hand-sized container.
- See individual chapters for the items needed for specific integration ceremonies.

Basic Set-Up for Ceremony

- Choose a private indoor or outdoor site for your ceremony.
- Build a Medicine Wheel using a representation for each of the Seven Sacred Directions (see the one described for the Ceremony of the East).
- Put the environment in order and have your journal at hand.
- Set Sacred Space.
- Smudge for clearing and cleansing.
- Review your intention.
- Say a prayer for protection.
- Request the presence of guides and other helpers.
- Ground, establish your connection to the Earth.

feet, and the space above your head. As you cleanse, focus your attention on releasing negativity of all kinds; use a prayer or other words (silently, or aloud if you wish) that invoke your own power of protection and cleansing.

Smudging can also include a ceremonial bath or shower. Or, you can use a feather with or without smoke in the same manner as described above. In addition, you can sprinkle water over your head with a small tree branch, or use a candle flame to bring light into your energy field, moving your hand from the flame toward yourself with an upward motion. The simplest smudging method is to use your hands to smooth and cleanse an energy field of interruptions, unwanted psychic debris, or outside energy forms.

Path of the White Wolf

Grounding

Inner work requires that you be centered and steady inside as you attune yourself to the voice within. Meditation, ceremony, and other rituals develop this ability. Before you begin any of these, always take a few moments to leave the outside world behind and ground yourself, becoming fully present and undistracted by worries or concerns.

1. Take a comfortable position, either sitting or lying down, and be still but not rigid.
2. Take a few deep, relaxing breaths, and imagine the tension draining from your body with each outbreath.
3. Begin to consciously relax parts of your body, one breath at a time: feet, legs, hips, chest, arms, hands, throat, jaw, eyes, skin, internal organs, etc. We find it helpful to focus on each body part or organ, and to say "relax," silently, to that part of the body. Take as long as you need in each area. If you begin to think about other things, just disengage from the thoughts and gently bring yourself back to your body.
4. Once your mental chatter subsides and you feel vibrantly present, relaxed, and calm, visualize yourself growing roots into

the Earth Mother (whatever that means for your physical situation). Feel her loving presence and support. Feel your connection to all that is. Acknowledge yourself as a sacred being.

5. Once centered or grounded and still, you are ready to focus on the task at hand.

Setting the Circle

Now you are ready to set your space by Calling the Circle. Some traditions refer to this practice as casting a Circle.

1. After smudging, ground and hold your intention clearly.

2. Stand in the center of the space where you'd like to do your work.

3. Turn completely around the space, using your hand or a sacred object to draw an imaginary circle of light around the perimeter of the area. You may also use cornmeal, ash from smudge, or sea salt to physically draw the circle perimeter.

4. If you wish, use a statement to enforce this act. It can be very simple, such as "I call this circle of protection for this sacred space. Let only that which is beauty, truth, and love enter here." An even simpler one: "Highest truth, greatest good, only love, harm to none." Tailor this to your individual needs.

When you are finished, this space will be a sacred refuge for as long as you wish to use it. If you are not in this space you can perform a ritual of protection for yourself anywhere and any time by visualizing yourself surrounded by a bright white light of protection, and calling on your guides to watch over you. See the section below on guides and helpers.

Visualization and Journeying

Visualization and journeying are key techniques that allow us to obtain information from the astral plane or dreamtime. You'll use these visionary practices often in the work you do on the Path of the White Wolf.

The visualizations offered in this book will teach you how to move through inner space to other realities. With this type of practice, you are guided to a particular place with a specific goal in mind. As you gain more experience, you will develop your own format for setting out on your inner voyage.

You may notice that the colors and shapes of trees, animals, mountains, seas, and rivers in the guided meditations can be quite different from what you find in your waking world. In this alternate reality landscape, sometimes called the dreamtime, your animal guides, or spirit guides in human, angelic, or other forms, may lead you to information. Each journey takes you through a part of the labyrinth of the invisible, until you reach a source that will impart knowledge and gifts which will aid you in the physical, day-to-day world.

You may find that when you begin using these techniques, you don't seem to "go" anywhere, or you may simply fall asleep. Don't worry. Stay with it. As you practice you will go deeper. Continue to prepare for journeying using the methods described in this chapter. Remember to set protection for yourself and to give yourself permission to end any journey that you don't feel ready to experience.

Journeying is similar to visualization, but it is usually directed by the inner guidance of the journeyer and his or her spirit helpers, with little instruction from an outside source. Journeyers enter a dreamtime/vision state, often through drumming, chant, and/or dance. The beat of the drum or the cadence of the chant or dance is the vehicle used by the journeyer to travel into other worlds, according to the cosmology of his or her culture, beliefs, traditions, personal visions or experiences, and dreams.

Shamanism and shamanic journeying are ancient healing arts originally ascribed to the Siberian *sha-ma,* or seer. Every tribal society throughout history has practiced some form of what we call shamanism. Even certain modern Christian denominations (the Pentecostals and Charismatics, for instance) practice a form of connection to the spirit world, through which they bring back information and guidance from the spiritual, invisible realms.

The ancient shamans were the forerunners of modern doctors and medicine men. They healed mind, body, and soul as they journeyed on behalf of the patient to the invisible realms, to non-ordinary reality, to retrieve lost parts of the patient's essence (soul or spirit retrieval). During these expeditions, they acquired information about herbal and other medicines with which to treat a particular ailment, and they sometimes fought spiritual battles with outside influences that were affecting the patient's spiritual, mental, emotional, or physical balance. As modern shamanic practitioners, we can obtain training to use these same techniques to assist our own and other's healing.

Typically, the sound of the drum holds the journeyer to the earthly plane and assists him or her in reaching and maintaining an alpha state in which altered realities become apparent. A change in drum tempo signals the time to return to normal consciousness. The drum rhythms used in shamanic practices vary from tribe to tribe and from purpose to purpose. A fast beat accesses beta waves and carries you into a trance state. According to your journey's purpose, different beats will facilitate the objective. You can find special drumming tracks to help you in your study and we encourage you to use them regularly.

Non-ordinary reality is typically described as comprising three distinct worlds.

- The Overworld or Upper World, which is the realm of the super-conscious, the angelic, the extraterrestrials, Father

Sky, creature beings, and spirit teachers. You may or may not recognize them, as many of them come from other star systems or have never manifested on Earth in physical form.

- The Underworld or Lower World is the abode of the subconscious and of the Earth Mother, and is inhabited by subterraneans, our personal power animals, and, sometimes, our ancestors.
- The Middle World is most closely akin to the world we see around us, more or less a parallel dimension to our three-dimensional, physical reality.

Your spirit guides and animal protectors may lead you through any or all of these worlds, according to your intention and what you need to experience on any given journey. In certain realms you may find help and assistance, but you may also find archetypal creatures whose purpose is to challenge or obstruct your journey. As in Aikido or any other martial art, often the way to fight such creations is by flowing around them, rather than engaging in attack.

As you explore the teachings in this book, the meditations will serve the role of guiding you into visualization and back again. To expand your journeying experience and learn additional skills, we also encourage you to seek out a teacher or guide to enhance your experience and education on the Path of the White Wolf. As you expand your practice beyond the guided meditations here, and begin to journey into non-ordinary reality in a more freeform way, it is important to seek direction and assistance from someone familiar with traversing non-ordinary reality and the worlds within. This teacher/mentor will set protection for your journey before you begin and will be there to help you understand and interpret what you are seeing—as well as being available to assist you in moving through each dimension with ease.

Guides from Other Realms and Other Helpers

You may connect with beings that seem to be watching over you and sharing wisdom with you. These helpers are called by many names: guardian angels, totem animals, personal guides, your own higher self, imaginary friends, relatives no longer of the earth plane (ancestors), your own previous incarnations, gods, or goddesses.

Sometimes these guides and helpers or entities accompany you long-term; sometimes they appear for only a short time of need. You instinctively know they mean you well, and you can sense their integrity; without question, you understand they are enlightened beings. On this path you will meet entities that will work with you during certain phases, bringing you information that you need to progress in your cycle of learning.

Occasionally you may encounter non-physical beings or entities (and also certain incarnate individuals on the earth plane) that do not mean you well. It is important to remember to set your personal protection at all times so that this is less likely to occur. If this does happen, call in your own guides again for protection, release the entity by sending it light and love, and seal yourself from it with your own protective light.

Infrequently, certain entities will not leave without outside help. In this case, we recommend that you look for a local Medicine Person or spiritual intuitive who can help discern what the entity is trying to fulfill through its attachment to you. The Medicine Person can then assist you in dealing with the situation.

Journaling

Journaling offers a handy and useful way to track your personal transformation. It is like keeping a travel diary. All it involves is taking the time to write down your visualizations, dreams, and journeys, and the teachings that resonate with you along the way. The physical act of writing gives form to your experience and connects you to the teaching in a deeper way. Writing is therapeutic and helps you physically release ideas, energy, and negativities. A written record helps clarify issues and highlight insights and understandings. This practice also serves to remind you of teachings and experiences in your transformation process that may only make sense months later.

If you find yourself resisting writing, we encourage you to think about why. Some reasons may be:

- **Privacy.** Are you afraid that someone else won't respect your journal?

- **Writing time**. What is your level of commitment to this work?

- **Takes too long**. Do you have a computer? Perhaps you could use your own form of shorthand.

- **Writing block**. Do you feel that you aren't a good writer? Consider using a tape recorder at first, and then later try writing at some point.

- **What's the point?** Do you feel that writing is not effective?

We invite you to be open to trying new methods as a part of the learning process. Change is good, and a healthy sense of adventure can transform your life!

If you still find that you cannot journal, try drawing a picture of your process. You can use the Medicine Wheel in the following way.

1. Draw a circle with four quadrants, with yourself in the East, your partner relationships in the South, your work and community relations in the West, and your contributions to the world in the North.

2. Remember to stay in the present moment as you draw, as simply or elaborately as you wish, what's going on for you NOW.

3. If this doesn't work, try dancing or singing your experience and feelings.

Remember, your process is only as effective as your ability to absorb and understand the teachings.

Working in Community

We all have a family, a village, a tribe: even if it's embodied only in our cat, the plants in our homes, or the trees outside our doors. As human beings, we need to share this journey with someone who loves us. Although many of the exercises in this book can only be done alone, sharing what you experience in some way will deepen it for you, make the journey less lonely, and offer support if you find yourself stuck in an uncomfortable stage.

The Tribe

In tribal situations, children were taught differently than we are taught as Westerners in modern culture. School was the great outdoors and teachers were aunties and uncles. Usually by the time a boy was six or seven, he was assigned to a skilled craftsman, usually an older relative, who could teach him the necessary skills of hunting, fishing, and perhaps the martial skills of a warrior/protector. He might also learn a trade, such as crafting arrowheads. A girl learned the art of basketry; how to sew hides, barks, and rushes for clothing, temporary shelter, or tipis, and other useful objects; and trained in the skill of finding, identifying, and preparing herbs for medicinal and ritual purposes.

Some boys learned to make medicine; some girls became warriors. There were "twin spirits" *(berdache)*, who carried the spirit of both a man and woman, and these people were considered sacred, often training to care for sacred items used in ceremony. Sometimes a dream of the thunder beings would proclaim one as a Heyokah, the sacred clown who taught by doing things backward. Each youngster, no matter what his or her calling, needed a mentor to help bring out the gifts given at birth or through dreams and visions. This way of teaching was very different than our modern methods.

Another teaching tool employed by our ancestors was that of storytelling. Children began to hear the tribal stories at birth, and over time the stories were expanded. Teaching was a circular motion—yet another teaching of the spiral. The storyteller would lead the children within, to the kernels of truth to be found in the story, and then back out again to the larger picture and the way the truths might be applied in their lives or the lives of those around them. The teaching was always backed by hands-on experience.

Each story had a multitude of meanings, and the children learned what was most pertinent to their life experiences. By the time they reached adulthood, they had gleaned much from each story or legend. This is archetypal learning, something we often miss in our current culture. In today's schools, ancient myths such as the Greek tragedies are studied more for their structure than their content. We miss much in this way, for an oft-repeated myth challenges our minds to find the hidden significance within the narrative.

The Value of the Village

Each person who studies the Path of the White Wolf will have a different experience. What is profound for one may be less important for another. Sharing experiences deepens your connection and interdependence with your community/tribe and village. While the written exercises were developed to do alone, if you anticipate that an exercise will bring discomfort, please find someone who can witness and support your work. You and your partner can change places, so that each receives encouragement.

As a society we have forgotten how to live together in nurturing support of each person's unique purpose. Without support and sustenance we can wander aimlessly, forgetting our purpose entirely; or we might get caught up in fulfilling someone else's purpose. As a result we sometimes work at jobs we hate, feeling as though we must do so in order to survive. We participate in activities that drain our energy, and form partnerships with people we don't really want to be with. We move into a downward spiral that leads to ambivalence, depression, despair—sometimes even to crimes against ourselves and others.

You can help repair this societal flaw by creating your own village, a tribe of friends, or a *tiyospaye,* an extended family. This family, which you choose, can be more supportive and fulfilling than a natal family.

For the purpose of this course, we recommend a group of no more than seven, with each person holding the place of one of the seven directions. Power increases exponentially with connection, concentration, and consolidation. As has been written: "Wherever two or more are gathered, I (the Great Mystery) shall be there." You may prefer to work in a group with all women or all men, or in a mixed group. Consider which environment will best support your growth. The group should include those who wish to delve deeply into themselves and the mysteries that will unfold with their participation. While one person may be elected as pathfinder to guide certain portions of each chapter's lesson plan, that person will be a servant rather than a leader.

Setting Up for
Group Meetings & Ceremonies

Your first group endeavor will be to choose a site on which to build a Medicine Wheel and a group altar. An outdoor setting is best, but an indoor area will work if it is relatively empty and large enough to comfortably hold the group. The drawing on the next page will give you an idea of ways to set up the sacred spaces you will need.

The set up will include three separate areas.

1. The group altar.
2. The Medicine Wheel.
3. The Village entry, including a gateway into the Medicine

Wheel and the altar. The altar referred to here is the group shrine, not the altar within the Medicine Wheel.

Ceremony Design

Ceremony is formally defined as an activity prescribed by custom, ritual, or religious belief that unites group members and celebrates accomplishments or milestones. In the chapter section on ceremony, "Honoring Sacred Elements," we've listed ceremonies that follow a set pattern common to the Path of the White Wolf. The facilitator of each event, in accordance with the way he or she was taught, will modify the format appropriately.

Path of the White Wolf

There are a few differences between ritual and ceremony, as practiced by native peoples. Generally, rituals are contained within ceremony, and there may be several ritual components in a complete ceremony. You will be conducting private or small group ceremonies for yourself or your tribe based on the recommendations for each lesson. These completion ceremonies celebrate the end of the teaching and provide a way to physically integrate each teaching. Their imagery and the emotions they evoke are powerful and transformative, elevating your understanding to another level.

For your group gatherings, set up your ceremonies simply or elaborately, as you desire. The more spontaneous you can be, the better. Spirit dwells in spontaneity. If you have a question, move into silence for a moment—the Great Mystery will speak to you in the pregnant pause of possibility.

Designing Group Ceremony

- Set sacred space.
- Call the Circle. If performed outside, spread cornmeal around the perimeter of the Medicine Wheel or Circle while inviting in all the helping spirits of those present, and invoking protection against unwanted presences. Include an opening prayer.

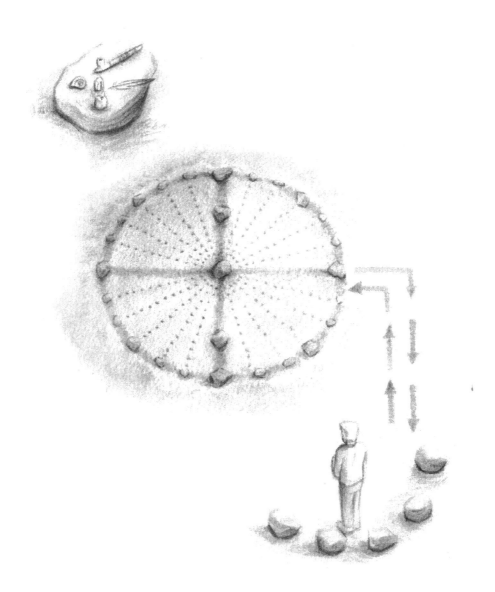

- Call in the directions. Use a drum and a chant, song, or prayer to acknowledge the Powers of each Direction (as noted in each chapter).
- Summon the ancestors and helpers of each person present. Each individual can do this, silently or aloud, as he or she leaves the Village area and steps into the Medicine Wheel Circle to participate in the ceremony. If it's a group ceremony, the pathfinder should smudge each person at this time, as well.
- Follow the guidelines for each ceremony. Sometimes there will be a meditation or visualization process included. See the pertinent chapter for ceremony guidelines. It is important to follow the formula outlined in each chapter, as each ceremony builds and expands on the previous ones.
- To close the Circle, the leader or pathfinder releases the ancestors, helpers, and Powers of each Direction with drumming and prayer. Leave an offering of beauty as a sign of respect and gratitude for what you have received.

Creating a Ceremony for the Tribe

Ceremony bonds members of the group and confers on each participant the power of the whole. Each of you will contribute in many ways to the success of this practice.

1. To begin, each person brings an item to the altar each time the tribe comes to Council to share a lesson. The item for the altar should be specific to the teachings of the direction, such as a representation of the animals found in your work in the direction, or the element the direction explores.

2. Place the altar away from the Medicine Wheel, facing the direction in which you are working. Make the altar area beautiful: it is the shrine of All-Who-Have-Come-Before-You, the ancestors, animal nations, star beings, and Creative Mind.

3. The group will meet in the region set aside for the Village. This section is removed from the Medicine Wheel and altar. It is a circular area where people can sit to discuss the chapter and share individual work completed before coming to the gathering.

4. When it is time to begin the ceremony, the pathfinder invites the tribe to proceed to the altar, find a comfortable position, and begin the meditation from the current study chapter.

   The pathfinder will need to
   - appoint someone to bring and operate the CD player.
   - stay aware of anyone who needs support throughout the meditation.
   - identify one or two group members to assist in whatever ways are needed.

5. When the meditation is finished, the tribe can spend a few minutes sharing experiences.

6. During this time, the pathfinder and helpers set up for ceremony. When they are ready, the group will choose members to take on the different roles incorporated in the ceremony: someone to drum and call in the Seven Directions, someone to smudge and/or light candles, etc.

7. Each group member will take a turn performing the specific ceremony prescribed for the direction. Allow each person to take as much time, make as much noise, experience as much emotion, and move around as much as he or she needs to. If, however, someone seems to be *really* out of control (this won't happen often), it is the responsibility of the pathfinder and helpers to take that person aside and offer gentle words, smudge, prayer, and chants to calm him. It is important to encourage the person and let him know that release through ceremony is a part of healing. It is also important to remind him that he has a choice about whether he wants to stay in the past story of his life or to let it go. It is also good to recommend a more conventional

method of counseling or support in addition to the work with the Wheel, especially for someone who has been deeply traumatized.

8. When the first member has completed his journey around the Wheel, the Village welcomes him back with loving support. Then the next person enters the Medicine Wheel and the journey begins again, until each person, including the pathfinder, has completed the ceremony.

9. You have now had sustenance and healing for the soul; it's time to nourish the body in comfort, love, and community celebration. Bring luscious food for a communal feast after the ceremony. This is essential. We can't tell you how many times we've been told to Feed the People. Enjoy this sharing of bread with one another. Feast, sing, dance, and express your joyful exuberance at the completion of this rite of passage.

Path of the White Wolf

Honoring Sacred Elements

The ceremonies we've outlined below are usually group rites, although many can be practiced solo. Group ceremony or ritual can be created for almost any occasion, as long as you maintain consideration for the participants and their respective belief systems, and ensure the safety of the group and individuals. Until you have a significant history of experience under your belt, we do not recommend that you facilitate ceremony for any groups except your study group, especially with people you don't know. The energy dynamics in a group ceremony can be unpredictable, and you do not want to be responsible for someone getting hurt at an event that went awry. We cannot stress this enough: It can be dangerous to use medicine tools and rituals without full understanding of the ways that these powers can affect other lives.

In the same way, we recommend that before you participate in any event, you find out about the facilitators and their experience. Although you have the tools to protect yourself, choose events and facilitators carefully before putting yourself in a potentially unpleasant or uncontrolled situation.

Medicine Circle

This is one of the first ceremonial events attended by most people. A Medicine Circle, or Sacred Circle, is called when two or more people wish to come together for a specific intention. The intention may be prayer, healing, witnessing someone's rite of passage, or an invitation to join in Council. To initiate Sacred Circle is to set intention, clear the space through smudging, call in the ancestors and the directional Powers for protection and guidance, and set the boundaries and guidelines that must be honored during the time that the Circle is meeting. It is disrespectful to interrupt or intrude upon a Circle that is in session. You must wait for an invitation, and if you don't receive one, you should leave.

Making Right Circle

This Medicine Circle is called specifically to promote healing between two or more people who are in disagreement. Often, an elder mediates this Circle. Once the Circle has been set and the intention agreed upon, each person is given a specific amount of time to tell his or her viewpoint of the event in question, without interruption. If there is a mediator, his or her purpose is to make sure each person is allowed to speak freely, and then to give suggestions for possible solutions to the problem. Before the Circle ends, each person is asked if she is ready to embrace the other in healing. The elder then prays for the healing of all concerned, asking the ancestors and personal guides to help them find the truth of their connections to themselves and each other.

Council Lodge

This is a Sacred Circle of Peers called to discuss needs, problems and solutions, resources, and the events for a community. The guidelines for the Medicine Circle apply here. Usually, a Council Lodge is conducted by selected elders, an equal number from both genders if it is a mixed community. This Circle may last for days, and is served and witnessed by the community at large. Many rituals may take place over the duration of the Council. Decisions are made by consensus, not the vote of the majority, so items on the agenda that are not resolved are tabled for the next Council Lodge. Often, the issues either disappear or resolve themselves between meetings.

Prayer Ties

Sometimes these are called Tobacco Ties because each one is filled with a pinch of tobacco. Prayer Ties are made with squares of cloth in the colors of each direction, then tied together about two inches apart with a piece of string. As you cut the cloth in a three- or four-inch square, then fill it with tobacco, you pray for your intention according to the direction of that color. In other words, in the East you will pray for illumination about your intention, in the South you will ask for trust that your need will be met, and so on. Prayer Ties are used primarily for Sweat Lodge and Vision Quest, but occasionally a tie of any color is made to set on an altar to hold intention for a prayer.

Pipe

Many tribes believe in the sacredness of the Pipe and tobacco. The Sioux Pipe was given to the tribe by White Buffalo Calf Woman many centuries ago, and is now carried by nineteenth-generation caretaker Arvol Looking Horse. Sioux Pipes are called *chanupas*, and are always made from catlinite, which is found in the sacred quarries of Pipestone. Other tribes have Pipes made of clay and different types of stones. A few use antler, but these are usually tourist pipes and are toxic to smoke. If you have one, please do not use it as anything other than ornamentation.

It is a huge responsibility to be a Pipe Carrier, and one that has to be authorized by a Native American elder. Robin, who carries both a Sioux Sundance Pipe and her Okanagon great-grandmother's Pipe, tells us that Pipe Carriers must go anywhere that prayer is requested, whenever someone calls for the Pipe. It is taught that whatever you pray for with the Pipe will be given to you, so you'd better watch what you pray for!

Each tribe has a traditional way of loading the Pipe and traditional prayers that are said with it. If you have not been trained in the use of the Pipe, please do not buy one in a store and think that you can make up your own ritual. If you already have a Pipe and have not been trained, find someone who can teach you. They will pray with you and help you to determine if the Way of the Pipe is for you. Until then, you may not know enough to be able to use the Pipe as a carrier for all the people.

Sweat Lodge

This is the Ceremony of Purification. In the Okanagon way, the Sweat Lodge is called *Quilsten*, and the poles of the Lodge are Creator's ribs. When The People enter the Lodge, they enter the heart of the Creator. The floor of the Lodge represents the Womb of the Mother, and the union of the Father and Mother is the Divine Marriage. This is the place to pray for the realization of your heart's true desires. In the Sioux way, the ceremony is called *Inipi*. The door of the Okanagon Lodge is in the West, for healing. This is the direction that starts the ceremony. In the Sioux tradition, the door is set in the East for illumination. Whatever direction begins the Lodge, the traditional way is to pray in four rounds, one to each direction, keeping in mind the Powers of that Direction.

A traditional Native American Sweat Lodge is constructed of 12 to 16 willow sapling poles. One end of each pole is staked into the ground, bent over in a dome shape, and tied in the center to its opposite pole, creating a circle. A Lodge can be large enough for 20 people or small enough for two. A shallow pit, about a foot deep, is dug out of the center of the space within the Lodge. Up to 100 dry stones are gathered. The stones are heated in a sacred fire. (Do not use stones from a riverbed or water source as they can explode and hurt someone badly.) At the beginning of each round, a number of stones, specified by the person pouring the Sweat, are brought into the pit in the center of the Lodge. Next, a bucket of water is brought in for pouring on the rocks after each prayer. This creates the steam of purification. Certain sacred herbs are brushed on the hot stones to create Prayer Smoke. This ceremony should only be led by someone who has been initiated in the way of the tribe with which he or she associates, and who has been trained through apprenticeship to pour water. Many things can happen in a Sweat Lodge, because people come to a Lodge to do deep healing work. A well-meaning but inexperienced leader would not have the wisdom to take care of all the participants, and the outcome could be unpleasant, even dangerous. Therefore, it is very important to find out who is leading a Sweat Lodge and what his qualifications are. If a leader doesn't ask if new people are present who have not Sweat before, and does not present teachings about his Lodge protocols before you enter, we recommend you carefully consider whether you wish to participate inside the Lodge. You can always pray around the fire. If you know the leader and are comfortable with his or her energy and ability to respond to anything that may arise, then do attend. Each Lodge is different, and each Lodge experience is an opportunity to commune with spirit and emerge reborn

Life Transition and GiveAway

These are often called Rites of Passage Ceremonies. In tribal cultures, certain events trigger the need for an initiatory experience witnessed by the community, to help a person make a transition to the next phase of life. A new birth is occasion for such a ceremony, as is new menses for a young woman or the beginning of adolescence for a boy. Other events that call for ritual are weddings, loss of a loved one, and entering the "Lodge of the Elders."

Entering the Lodge of the Elders is an honoring ceremony that marks an important life transition in traditional indigenous cultures that value the contribution of elders. This transition occurs for women when they hold their wise blood and take up a more formal teaching/healing role in the community. (Western culture calls this menopause.) For men, this occurs when their experience and wisdom are sought more often than their physical ability, announcing their passage into sagehood. (We in the West call this retirement.)

Rituals like these, supported by community, are an important aspect of indigenous culture that has for the most part been lost in the modern world. In Western culture, birthday parties, graduations, retirement parties, baptisms, and bar mitzvahs serve a similar purpose.

A significant element of the Life Transition Ceremony is the GiveAway. Generally speaking, in our present culture, witnesses give gifts to friends and loved ones in celebration of life transitions. In traditional cultures, the opposite occurs. The person in transition gives to others as a means of shedding the old to make way for the new—a transformation in every facet of life.

GiveAway, while central to the Life Transition Ceremony, plays a role in almost every Native American ceremony: from the Interior Salish tradition of Winter Dance, the Northwest Coastal people's Potlatch, the Pueblo clan's Kiva ceremonies, the Plains tribes' Sun Dance, to an intertribal PowWow. The power of GiveAway is universal.

Seasonal

Indigenous people worldwide celebrate the changing of the seasons, offering their gratitude for the blessings of each. Often such ceremonies are performed at the quarter marks of the year: equinox and solstice. Spring rituals may include planting (corn is one of the main staples for Native Americans); summer may be a ritual offering to the sun; fall is a harvesting ritual in which gratitude is expressed to and for all the bearing plants; and winter's rituals may include the dreamtime. Each tribe or community develops its own rituals as part of the overall ceremony, and with repetition these ceremonies become part of the common tradition.

Moon

There are many practices for "Drawing Down the Moon." In some cultures, the moon is the Grandmother, married to Grandfather Sun. She is his reflection, and controls the ebb and flow of the tides of life. Her power is necessary for the new growth of plant life and for women on their menses (also called a woman's "moon time"), and it nurtures both individual and collective energies. Most tribal people dance the Full Moon, and in many societies the women gather at the dark of the moon to bury their menstrual flow and the placenta from childbirth, and to plant new corn and other crops.

Vision Quest

This ceremony has been held throughout the indigenous world since time immemorial. In Okanagon life, a child who reached the age of puberty was sent out over a one- or two-night period to find his *tamanohwis,* or guardian spirit power. The Sioux call it *hanblecya,* crying for a vision, while Aborigines sent young adolescents on Walk About. Vision Quest is the way tribal people search out their life purpose. It's also the way many people become acquainted with their spirit helpers, guides, and totems.

In general, a Vision Quest consists of going alone to a preferred spot in nature (one where you will not be disturbed by other humans), casting a sacred Circle, divesting yourself of clothing and other accoutrements (no tents allowed!), and fasting, although many people today take water with them. The intention is to stay in silence and prayer within the Circle, without eating, for up to four days. While some people do this on their own, it is preferable to ask a Medicine Person to "put you on the hill." This leader will pray with and for you, tend a sacred fire for your strength, and support your intention, and will await the end of your journey with the offering of a Sweat Lodge for your purification. He or she will then assist you to interpret any signs, dreams, visions, or encounters you experienced.

Moon Lodge

In villages where women lived and worked together, most women's menses came at the same time each month, according to the cycle of the moon. The women came together in the Moon Lodge for the duration of their menses, to share crafts, stories, and teachings. The moon time is the time of a woman's greatest power, and this sacred Circle was a time for prayer and discussion of community needs. Women are at their most vulnerable during their moon, and also most susceptible to the opening of the crack between the worlds. It is a time for deep introspection and communication with other worlds. In traditional societies, the men cooked and took care of the children during a woman's moon.

Today women are often taught to be ashamed of menses, which fosters sickness. When women understand their true heritage, much of the pain and discomfort of menstruation disappears. It is especially beneficial for women in Western culture to set aside sacred time during menses, and to receive the gifts of community with each other.

Sun Dance

The version of the Sun Dance with which most people are acquainted originated with the Lakota Sioux. This four-day rite of endurance, sacrifice, and thanksgiving requires a high degree of intention and training. To be a Sun Dancer, one must make a four-year commitment and follow the disciplines required by the Sun Dance intercessor.

The Sun Dance is performed within a sacred arbor: a circle of limbed pine trees with a partial roof of pine or cedar boughs. Elders and supporters sit or stand under the arbor. In the center of the arbor, beneath the open sky, stands a forked cottonwood tree representing the Tree of Life. To the tree are tied Tobacco Ties from all the people, as effigies representing male and female. The Sun Dancers dance in the middle, directly under the sun. At some time during the dance (this varies with the tribe initiating the ceremony), the Sun Dance Chief pierces each male dancer on the chest just above the nipple and inserts a piece of wood just under the skin. A rope is then fastened to the wood via small thongs and also affixed to the center tree, while the dancer continues dancing.

Sun Dancers do not eat or drink for the four days and nights of the dance. When the dancer reaches a state of communion with the

guidance of the other world, he breaks away from the Tree of Life by
dancing backward, creating enough tension on the rope ties to pull
the wood from his skin. His sacrifice is a prayer for the safety and
abundance of all his people, especially the family that sponsors him.
In most Sun Dances, women do not pierce, as they already give of
their blood through childbirth and menses.

While some people call the Sun Dance ceremony "barbaric," we
cannot agree. Each dancer offers the only thing one really has to
give—the flesh—in a sacred dance that supports the life of all.

The Sun Dance is a once yearly occasion whose purpose is
to replenish the people and the Earth. The women dancers and
other supporters extend their full intention, lending strength and
courage to the men. It is one of the most beautiful examples of
community involvement ever to be witnessed. At the end of the
ceremony, a huge feast of traditional and not-so-traditional foods
is served, and all the dancers run from the end of the proces-
sional line to begin the feast and celebration.

Glossary

Aho Mitakuye Oyasin – Lakota term for All My Relations.

Akashic Records – Chronicles of the universe that have been stored in the stars since before the beginning of time; the history of the Earth and all Earth beings.

All [My] Our Relations – All Earth's children: winged ones, swimming ones, four-legged animals, plant and tree people, creepy-crawlers, stone people, our ancestors, and our descendents—seven generations back and seven generations forward. All known and unknown, all within sacred connection, the interdependent whole of the families of Mother Earth.

Black Elk – Deceased Lakota holy man whose remarkable visions have been an inspiration to many.

Blue Road – Line connecting the East and West directions that signifies the joining of spirit and matter; the Blue Road of spiritual attainment.

Ceremony – The ceremony at the end of each chapter is a way to integrate each of the lessons; it helps us embody the teachings in everything we do.

Chakras – Seven energy centers within the human body, as described in Eastern philosophies; these are spirit, mind, throat, heart, will, creative center, and root.

Circle – A spiritual gathering with a specific intention. The intention may be prayer, healing, witnessing someone's rite of passage, or an invitation to join in Council. To initiate Sacred Circle is to set intention, clear the space by smudging, and call in the ancestors and the directional Powers for protection and guidance.

Color – Indigenous people believe that the vibrations of color have potential healing power. Colors are also symbolic of the phases and directions of our lives, and they correspond to our chakras (energy centers).

Creatures – In Native American traditions and many others, the animal tribes were considered to be people, with nations of their own. Many stories speak about the time when animals talked, and they relate ways that animals offered to help foolish humans to live in balance on the Earth.

DNA – Deoxyribonucleic acid; the substance from which human genes are fashioned and the transmitter of inherited characteristics.

Dreaming – An altered state where the dreamer experiences alternative realities existing outside our everyday time and space limitations.

Earth Mother – Mother Earth is the womb from which we come. She is found Below the Medicine Wheel, the supporting foundation providing All Our Relations and each of us with all that we need to live.

Element – The element is the rudimentary physical principle used to describe each direction. Generally, Westerners consider only four elements: earth, air, water, and fire. Asian traditions use two more, wood and metal, and African tribalists call on the element of the mineral peoples (stones).

Embodiment – The embodiment is the way that we humans experience the aspects of each direction. Eastern people usually associate five or six of these attributes in their personality matrices. In this book, we use seven.

Emotion – The pervasive feeling often associated with a direction.

Expression – A physical way of putting our beliefs into action and giving them creative form.

Father Sky – Above the Wheel lies the realm of time-without-time: Sky Father, the keeper of Great Mystery. This is where we find sun, moon, stars, and the great unknown of the void.

Four-legged – Animal kingdom; those who walk on four legs.

Gifting – Practice of tithing, or of compensating those who nurture your spirit.

Great Mystery – That which is without definition, the unknown, and yet the creative source from which we come and of which we are an integral part.

Grounding or Grounded – Act of finding stillness and becoming fully present, undistracted by outside thoughts, worries, or concerns.

Guides – Beings that seem to be watching over you and sharing wisdom with you. These helpers are called by many names: guardian angels, totem animals, personal guides, your own higher self, imaginary friends, relatives no longer of the earth plane (ancestors), your own previous incarnations, gods or goddesses, etc.

Hanblecya – Lakota term for "crying for a vision" with humbleness. Also called Vision Quest.

Heyokah – Name given to those individuals whose visions impel them to see life and situations in contrast to the majority. They may actually seem backward; they may act or say the exact opposite of what they mean. Heyokah shows us alternative perspectives, most often in a humorous manner—like the trickster Coyote—so we can cleanse ourselves with the medicine of laughter and learn something new.

Higher self – Also called our essence, what some call the oversoul; the part of us that is spirit in body.

Inipi – Purification ceremony given to the people by White Buffalo Calf Pipe Woman; also called Sweat Lodge.

Integration – The act of assimilating what we've experienced, bringing it within ourselves to a deeper understanding.

Intention – The act of consciously and clearly setting your mind to your objective. The simpler and more concise you can get it, the better.

Journeying – A form of meditation/visualization that entails traveling through one's inner landscapes to the middle, upper, or lower worlds, held to the earthly plane only by the sound of the drum. Drumming assists participants in reaching and maintaining an alpha state more receptive to altered realities; journeyers are signaled to return by a change in tempo.

Lakota – A tribe of peoples, also called Sioux, who live in the Dakotas.

Lesson – Each direction illustrates a certain set of lessons that will carry forward throughout our lives, or for this cycle of learning.

Medicine – Gifts from spirit with which all beings are endowed; these manifest in a unique and special way for each of Earth's children.

Medicine Bundle – Sacred package or bag containing items that hold special meaning or power; usually the gifts of spirit, teachers, or the Earth herself.

Medicine person/teacher – Sometimes called shaman. A medicine person helps others with healing, transformation, and understanding.

Medicine Shield – Image or article that integrates special symbols and designs which hold special meaning or power; usually the gifts of spirit, teachers, or the Earth herself.

Medicine Wheel – Circle of stones, found in many places in North America, Canada, and around the world. These Circles were placed with care on sacred ground by indigenous peoples. The Wheel was used for ceremony and ritual, and was known to have great power to initiate change and healing. The stone Wheel represents the wheel of life, encompassing all that is, and illustrates the connection of every aspect.

Moon cycle – It has been understood for centuries that a woman's menstrual cycle is associated with the phase of the moon. If women live together in community, they will eventually experience their monthly cycles within a few days of each other. Even the oceans ebb and flow with the cycles of the moon.

Moon Lodge – Women's ceremonial retreat time. In villages where women lived and worked together, most women's menses came at the same time each month, according to the cycle of the moon. The women came together in the Moon Lodge for the duration to share crafts, stories, and teachings. This moon time is the time of a woman's greatest power, and this sacred circle was a time for prayer and discussion of community needs, as well as a time for deep introspection and communication with Other Worlds.

Mother Earth – See Earth Mother.

Okanagon / Okanagan – Native peoples who inhabit the central Columbia Plateau of British Columbia and Central Washington.

Other Side Camp – Dwelling place of those who have passed on from the earthly plane and wait for us in the spirit world.

Phase of life – Just as the sun and moon have cycles, so do we. We begin at birth, move through childhood and adulthood, and into our elder years. Each stage is unique and has its own learnings.

Pipe – Sacred ceremony and implements given to the people by White Buffalo Calf Woman many centuries ago; it is now carried by nineteenth-generation caretaker Arvol Looking Horse. Sioux Pipes are called *chanupas* and are always made from catlinite, found in the sacred quarries in Pipestone, Minnesota.

Place on the Wheel – We always return to the place of beginning. This is our truth. But truth without experience is very weak. We must journey around the Wheel, stopping in each Sacred Direction, in order to strengthen our ability to stand in our truth.

Pleiades – Loose cluster of stars in the direction of the constellation Taurus. Named after the Seven Sisters of Greek mythology, these stars appear to be surrounded by a keen nebulosity that shines by their reflected light.

Prayer Bundle – Medicine bundle used to represent certain prayers, often used with prayer arrows.

Red Road – Line connecting the North and South directions, the union of creativity and wisdom; the Red Road of the physical plane.

Sacred Hoop – The energy that encompasses all beings and the

Path of the White Wolf

Earth; the circle of life that holds all that is and All Our Relations.

Sacred space – The environment within which you can do spiritual work; it includes creating an environment, a place that is blessed, and it allows you to focus on the work at hand.

Seasons – Seasons have been astrologically related to the directions of the Medicine Wheel since time began. Tribal astronomers often used Medicine Wheels to determine the changing of the seasons.

Seven Sacred Directions – The four cardinal directions—East, South, West, and North—as well as the three center directions—Above, Below, and Center.

Shaman – Siberian word for someone who journeys into non-ordinary reality to serve community by acting as a healer or medicine person. This term is often applied to any medicine person, regardless of tradition. One traditional practice of shamanism includes entering a dreamtime/vision state through drumming, chant, and/or dance.

Sky Father – See Father Sky.

Smudge – The act of ritually cleansing an object, an energy field, or an area such as a room. Personal smudging is often done to prepare for inner work or ceremony. A common way of smudging is to use the smoke from herbs such as sage, cedar, or sweetgrass burned loose in a fired earthen bowl or a shell, or as a tied bundle (smudge stick). Pass the smoke through your energy field, your front torso, your backside, the soles of feet, and above your head. Focus your attention on cleansing; use a prayer or sacred words if you wish (silently or aloud).

Standing Ones – Ancient trees, who have stood for longer than any other living being.

Star Nations – Those who come from the sky. Many indigenous peoples have stories of beings who came from Star Nations.

Subterraneans – Those who live below the earth; they aerate the soil, enrich the humus, and fertilize the plant people.

Sun Dance – Four-day renewal rite of endurance, sacrifice, and thanksgiving; held in the summer among many northern Native American tribes.

Sweat Lodge – See Inipi.

Time – The time of day or night is important because each phase of the sun/moon dial carries with it a certain type of power. These powers can be called upon to aid us in our endeavors.

Tiyospaye – Lakota term for our own village tribe of friends and/ or family; an extended family; our tribe of affinity.

Totem animals – Also called power animals, totem animals act as our guards and guides.

Tsalgi – Cherokee peoples.

Turtle Island – Native name for North America; derived from creation stories recounting that mud from the floor of the great oceans was placed on the back of a great turtle.

Vision Quest – See Hanblecya.

Way – Pathway we follow in learning about the powers we can receive through each direction.

White Buffalo Calf Pipe Woman – White Buffalo Calf Pipe Woman brought the gift of the sacred Pipe and other ceremonies to the Lakota (Sioux) peoples. Throughout time her story has been told to remind the people of the sacredness of life and that we must walk the Earth in a good way, in balance with All Our Relations.

Wotai – Cherokee term for small stone.

Index

Acknowledgments

We owe a debt of deep gratitude to those who taught us to walk the path of Beauty. For many years Robin followed the Sun Dance Way and her own people's Winter Dance. Martin High Bear, Sun Dance Chief, was a man of great strength, vision, and wisdom. Sandy and Robin learned the healing songs and ceremonies with Northwest Coastal Salish teachers and healers Fred Beaver Chief Jameson and Johnny Moses. Hopi messenger Thomas Banyacya shared the prophecies and taught us to be humble. Siberian Shaman Grandmother Mingo, Grandfather Misha, and his niece, Nadyashta Duvan shared the teachings of the Kamlanya.

Robin has been deeply touched by the Huna teachings of L'au Lapa'au, Henry Awae, Aunties Pua, Mahealani, Nahi Gutzman of the Hawaiian nation, and by Hinewhirangi, Nga Tai, and Raina Ferriis of the Maori Iwis. Peruvian Shaman Don José and Aboriginal elder Gagadju shared the wonders of the Plant Medicine world. Among Robin's wonderful women teachers are her mother, Charlotte, and her adopted mother, Edythe Wildshoe Hardman; her grandmothers, Lucille Raymond (Okanagon) and Cubal Youngblood (Tsalagi); great-grandmother Salmiac (Okanagon), who transmits from the Other Side Camp; Karen Timentwa, her grandmother, Mrs. Lum (Okanagon/Sioux), and Sahn Ashinna (Navajo/Blackfoot).

Sandy has been blessed with the opportunity to learn from the incredible women teachers who travel to the Pacific Northwest for the annual Women of Wisdom conference, including Brooke Medicine Eagle, Nicki Scully, Jamie Sams, Riane Eisler, Angeles Arrien, and Ruth Barrett. Sandy also sends her deepest gratitude to Wabun Wind and Dawn Songfeather Davies, who held up the sign to the Red Road many years ago; to Mariah Rose, Neesah Heart, Joy Tunnell, Uncle Walt Hosel, and Sage Stone for their heartfelt teaching and wisdom; and to her mother, Teresa D'Entremont, without whom this book would not have been possible.

And lastly, we send our sincere appreciation to the CeciBooks team for their inspiration, patience, and hard work, and for helping produce this book in all its beauty.

Tsonkwondiyonrat! (We are all One Spirit!)

About the Authors

Robin Tekwelus Youngblood

Robin Tekwelus Youngblood writes, "As an Okanagon/Tsalagi (Cherokee), I have been a student of my heritage for many years, studying with indigenous elders of my own tribes, along with Siberian and Aboriginal shamans. I have learned so much from these honored elders—teaching, prophecy, ritual, ceremony, song and dances to balance our lives and our planet. Over the years I have found myself in the position of being a bridge between Native American traditions and European cultures. I've been told that it is now time to share the things that have been passed on to me—and, out of respect for our tribal ways, what I now teach is a synthesis of ancient knowledge and contemporary practices."

Sandy D'Entremont

Coauthor Sandy D'Entremont is a sacred fire-keeper and ceremonial singer. She has been a student of earth-based spiritual practices for over 25 years and blends the principles of many traditions into the Universal Medicine Wheel. Her work in community focuses on supporting women's circles and women's ceremony, holding the container of the circle to foster initiation and transition. She is known for her ability to lend a calming clarity and focus to facilitate communication, understanding, and healing.

Printed in Great Britain
by Amazon